6th

Science
Daily Practice Workbook
20 weeks of fun activities

ARGOPREP

 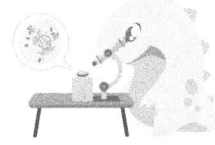  

Physical Science • **Life Science** • **Earth & Space Science** • **Engineering**

ArgoPrep is one of the leading providers of supplemental educational products and services. We offer affordable and effective test prep solutions to educators, parents and students. Learning should be fun and easy! To access more resources visit us at www.argoprep.com.

Our goal is to make your life easier, so let us know how we can help you by e-mailing us at: info@argoprep.com.

- ArgoPrep is a recipient of the prestigious **Mom's Choice Award**.

- ArgoPrep also received the 2019 **Seal of Approval** from Homeschool.com for our award-winning workbooks.

- ArgoPrep was awarded the 2019 **National Parenting Products Award**, **Gold Medal Parent's Choice Award** and **the Tillywig Brain Child Award**.

SCIENCE SERIES

Science Daily Practice Workbook by ArgoPrep is an award-winning series created by certified science teachers to help build mastery of foundational science skills. Our workbooks explore science topics in depth with ArgoPrep's 5 E'S to build science mastery: Engaging, Exploring, Explaining, Experimenting, and Elaborating. All of our curriculum is aligned with the latest Next Generation Science Standards.

Introduction

Welcome to our 6th grade science workbook!

This workbook is for 6th grade students studying the Next Generation Science Standards. Included are 20 weeks of comprehensive instruction, working through the four branches of science: **Physical Science, Life Science, Earth and Space Science and Engineering.**

This workbook dedicates several weeks of instruction to each of the four branches of science, focusing on different standards within each week of instruction.

Within the branch of Physical Science, students will study Newton's Third Law, potential and kinetic energy, state of matter and waves. In Life Science, they will learn more about parts of a cell, photosynthesis and ecosystems. Students will dive into fossils, rocks, and seafloor structures in Earth and Space Science.

Finally, in the Engineering section, they will have the opportunity to become an engineer by creating and evaluating design solutions, generating data, and then analyzing the data. At the conclusion of the 20 weeks of instruction, students should have a solid grasp on the concepts required of the Next Generation Science Standards for 6th grade.

Table of Contents

How to Use the Book

All 20 weeks of daily activity pages in this book follow the same weekly structure. The book is divided into four sections: Physical Science, Life Science, Earth & Space Science and Engineering. The activities in each of the sections align to the Next Generation Science Standards which will help prepare students for state standardized assessments. While the sections can be completed in any order, it is important to complete each week within the section in chronological order, as the skills often build upon one another.

Each week focuses on one specific topic within the section. More information about the weekly structure can be found in the Weekly Planner section.

How to access video explantions?

Download our app:
ArgoPrep Video Explanations
to access videos on any mobile device or tablet.

or

Visit our website at:
www.argoprep.com/science6

Go to **argoprep.com/science6**
OR scan the QR Code:

Weekly Planner

Day	Activity	Description
1	Engaging with the Topic	Read a short text on the topic and answer multiple choice questions.
2	Exploring the Topic	Interact with the topic on a deeper level by collecting, analyzing, and interpreting data.
3	Explaining the Topic	Make sense of the topic by explaining and beginning to draw conclusions about the data.
4	Experimenting with the Topic	Investigate the topic through hands-on, easy to implement experiments.
5	Elaborating on the Topic	Reflect on the topic and use all information learned to draw conclusions and evaluate results.

List of Topics

Unit	Week	Topic
Physical Science	1	Newton's 3rd Law
Physical Science	2	Energy: Kinetic & Potential Energy
Physical Science	3	Energy: Thermodynamics
Physical Science	4	Energy of Molecules
Physical Science	5	Wave Energy in Technology
Life Science	6	Cell Theory
Life Science	7	Inheritance of Traits
Life Science	8	Energy Flow through Organisms
Life Science	9	Resource Availability in Ecosystems
Life Science	10	Interactions Between Organisms
Earth and Space Sciences	11	Geologic Time Scale
Earth and Space Sciences	12	Rock Layers
Earth and Space Sciences	13	Changing Earth
Earth and Space Sciences	14	Pangaea & Seafloor Spreading
Earth and Space Sciences	15	Natural Resources
Engineering	16	Identifying a Problem
Engineering	17	Developing a Solution
Engineering	18	Drafting and Redesigning Based on Data
Engineering	19	Developing a Model and Testing
Engineering	20	Evaluating, Redesigning, and Modifying

Next Generation Science Standards Correlation Guide

Unit	Next Generation Science Standard	Topic	Description of Standard
Physical Science	1	MS-PS2-1	Apply Newton's Third Law to design a solution to a problem involving the motion of two colliding objects.
Physical Science	2	MS-PS3-1	Construct and interpret graphical displays of data to describe the relationships of kinetic energy to the mass of an object and the speed of an object.
Physical Science	3	MS-PS3-3	Apply scientific principles to design, construct, and test a device that either minimizes or maximizes thermal energy transfer.
Physical Science	4	MS-PS1-4	Develop a model that predicts and describes changes in particle motion, temperature, and state of a pure substance when thermal energy is added or removed.
Physical Science	5	MS-PS4-1	Use mathematical representations to describe a simple model for waves that includes how the amplitude of a wave is related to the energy in a wave.
Life Science	6	MS-LS1-1&2	Conduct an investigation to provide evidence that living things are made of cells; either one cell or many different numbers and types of cells. Develop and use a model to describe the function of a cell as a whole and ways parts of cells contribute to the function.
Life Science	7	MS-LS3-2	Develop and use a model to describe why asexual reproduction results in offspring with identical genetic information and sexual reproduction results in offspring with genetic variation.

Unit	Next Generation Science Standard	Topic	Description of Standard
Life Science	8	MS-LS1-6	Construct a scientific explanation based on evidence for the role of photosynthesis in the cycling of matter and flow of energy into and out of organisms.
Life Science	9	MS-LS2-1	Analyze and interpret data to provide evidence for the effects of resource availability on organisms and populations of organisms in an ecosystem.
Life Science	10	MS-LS2-2	Construct an explanation that predicts patterns of interactions among organisms across multiple ecosystems.
Earth and Space Sciences	11	MS-ESS1-4	Construct a scientific explanation based on evidence from rock strata for how the geologic time scale is used to organize Earth's 4.6 billion-year-old history.
Earth and Space Sciences	12	MS-ESS2-1	Develop a model to describe the cycling of Earth's materials and the flow of energy that drives this process.
Earth and Space Sciences	13	MS-ESS2-2	Construct an explanation based on evidence for how geoscience processes have changed Earth's surface at varying time and spatial scales.
Earth and Space Sciences	14	MS-ESS2-3	Analyze and interpret data on the distribution of fossils and rocks, continental shapes, and seafloor structures to provide evidence of the past plate motions.
Earth and Space Sciences	15	MS-ESS3-1	Construct a scientific explanation based on evidence for how the uneven distributions of Earth's mineral, energy, and groundwater resources are the result of past and current geoscience processes.

Unit	Next Generation Science Standard	Topic	Description of Standard
Engineering	16	MS-ETS1-1	Define the criteria and constraints of a design problem with sufficient precision to ensure a successful solution, taking into account relevant scientific principles and potential impacts on people and the natural environment that may limit possible solutions.
Engineering	17	MS-ETS1-2	Evaluate competing design solutions using a systematic process to determine how well they meet the criteria and constraints of the problem.
Engineering	18	MS-ETS1-3	Analyze data from tests to determine similarities and differences among several design solutions to identify the best characteristics of each that can be combined into a new solution to better meet the criteria for success.
Engineering	19	MS-ETS1-4	Develop a model to generate data for iterative testing and modification of a proposed object, tool, or process such that an optimal design can be achieved.
Engineering	20	MS-ETS1-4	Develop a model to generate data for iterative testing and modification of a proposed object, tool, or process such that an optimal design can be achieved.

WEEK 1

Physical Science

Newton's 3rd Law

MS-PS2-1

Apply Newton's Third Law to design a solution to a problem involving the motion of two colliding objects.

ARGOPREP

Directions: Read the text below. Then answer the questions that follow.

Discovering Newton's Third Law

Imagine a demolition derby. This is a competition where cars smash into each other and the car that survives until the end wins. As car #12 speeds toward its competitor, car #9, which has stalled out, everyone in the stands holds their breath...who will be the victor? Suddenly, there is a loud crash as the two vehicles collide at an alarming speed. You notice something strange. Not only did they crash into each other, but car #12 also bounced backwards after hitting car #9 which had flipped over twice from the impact.

This scenario is an example of a **transfer of energy** which means energy moved from one object to another object. This example also demonstrates **Newton's Third Law** which states that for every action, there is an equal and opposite reaction. In this case, the action was car #12 speeding toward its competitor and colliding with it. The reaction was car #9 receiving that energy and flipping over, as well as car #12 bouncing backwards. Fortunately, everyone is fine thanks to the protective roll cages inside the cars, but it leaves you wondering - does Newton's Third Law apply to other things besides cars?

1. What happened when the speeding car (car #12) smashed into the stationary car (car #9)?

   A. It exploded.

   B. Energy was transferred from car #12 to car #9

   C. Energy was transferred from car #9 to car #12

   D. Nothing

2. Rewrite Newton's Third Law:

3. In our scenario, which car is the source of most of the energy?

   A. Car #9

   B. Car #12

   C. Both vehicles

   D. None of the above

Yesterday you discovered that Newton's Third Law explains how two objects interact with each other. For every action, there is an equal and opposite reaction. Today you will explore how this law works in real life using objects in your own home.

Directions: Using that knowledge, read the activity directions below. Then answer the questions that follow.

Applying Newton's Third Law

Using two different kinds of balls or two matchbox cars, let's make an experiment to test Newton's Third Law. For your experiment, you want to test what was explained in the story from yesterday with your objects.

Materials:

1. 2 different balls or 2 matchbox cars
2. Tape measure or ruler
3. Piece of tape

Procedure:

1. Design: Set up the experiment. One object, object A, will remain stationary at point A. The other object, object B, will be placed 3 feet away at point B. Mark both points with a small piece of tape.

2. Hypothesis: What do you think will happen when you roll object A at object B to try to make them collide? Write your hypothesis here:

3. Test: Test your experiment by pushing object A so that it collides with object B.

4. Record: Measure the distance each object travelled from point B and record in the data table that follows.

5. Trials: Run three more trials, and fill in the measurements on the data table the same way for each trial.

6. Average: Once you have your measurements, take an average of your data by adding the measurements of your four trials together. Divide that sum by 4.

7. Conclusion: Using your data, answer the questions below.

Newton's Third Law Data Table

Record the data from your experiment here.

Test	Object A's distance from point B	Object B's distance from point B
1		
2		
3		
4		
Average		

1. Using the averages, which object moved farther, Object A or Object B?

   A. Object A

   B. Object B

2. Explain why Object A or B moved farther from Point A.

3. Did your result support your hypothesis?

   A. Yes

   B. No

Directions: Using your experiment from yesterday, think about how you applied Newton's Third Law. Then answer the questions below.

1. Using at least 5 sentences, explain how Newton's Third Law helps explain what happened in yesterday's experiment.

2. What could you do to improve your experiment? Think about parts of the experiment that were challenging or maybe inconsistent. If you had unlimited time, money and resources, how could you make the design of this experiment better?

You have spent several days exploring the concept of Newton's Third Law. Now it's time to see it in action! Today you will create an experiment that demonstrates Newton's Third Law by creating a small rocket!

DIY Exploding Newton Rocket Experiment

Background: In this experiment you will be mixing Alka Seltzer and water in a small film canister in order to make your rocket. When Alka Seltzer is mixed with water, it releases carbon dioxide. As the gas builds up, it creates pressure in the film canister. The pressure of the carbon dioxide inside the canister is so strong that eventually it causes the canister lid to pop off. This force will cause the canister to shoot up into the air like a rocket!

Directions for Exploding Newton Rocket Experiment:

Materials:

1. Two Film Canisters
2. Box of Alka Seltzer Tablets
3. Water
4. Meter Stick or Tape Measure
5. _____ (For your experiment, you will need to decide what other material you want to have the exploding film canister push against that will move away from it). Write your chosen object here, and make sure you have it before beginning.

Procedure:

1. First, test out the rocket. To do this, load an Alka Seltzer tablet into your canister, and add water until it is almost full. Quickly put the cap on tightly and flip it cap-side down onto the ground. Take a few steps back from it for safety. After a second or two, it should fill up with enough carbon dioxide gas in order to pop the lid off, shooting the canister into the air like a rocket.

2. Try changing the quantity of Alka Seltzer or water that you use until you get the best explosion possible. Make sure you wipe off the inside of the lid in between uses since it can affect the seal and explosion. Write your perfect ratio of Alka Seltzer to water here:

_____

_____

3. Compare doing your explosion with the lid up vs. down. How is the direction or movement of your rocket different? Write your observations here:

_____

_____

4. Sit the canister on its side and place it so the lid is next to a large rock or something heavy. Load the canister again and wait for it to pop. How is the direction or movement of the rocket different this time?

_____

_____

Today you will pull together everything you have discovered about Newton's Third Law to explain what happened in your experiment and draw conclusions about how this relates on a larger scale to the rest of the universe.

Directions: Answer the following questions..

1. Explain what happened in your experiment yesterday. How does this relate to Newton's Third Law?

2. In what part of this experiment could you see a transfer of energy? How do you know?

3. If you placed two film canisters across from each other and shot them toward each other, what do you think might happen? There are a few possible answers to this question.

4. Do you see that the reaction between water and Alka Seltzer provides the energy for your rocket?

   A. Yes

   B. No

5. Is energy required for Newton's Third Law?

   A. Yes

   B. No

WEEK 2

Physical Science

Energy:
Kinetic & Potential Energy

MS-PS3-1

Construct and interpret graphical displays of data to describe the relationships of kinetic energy to the mass of an object and to the speed of an object.

Directions: Read the text below. Then answer the questions that follow.

Discovering Kinetic and Potential Energy

Have you ever ridden a roller coaster? The anticipation when you're standing in line, the adrenaline rush as you are buckled in, and the thrill as you are catapulted off into motion all make for a thrilling experience. Aside from the initial motor to power you up the first hill, there are no other motors on a roller coaster since the rest of the energy is stored and released over and over again at each hill. No matter what kind of roller coaster you ride, it will follow the same basic laws of physics. Roller coasters need to build up **potential energy** at the beginning of the track so they have enough **kinetic energy** to make it through all of the hills, twists, and turns to the end of the ride. Potential Energy (PE) is stored energy, or energy of position, and Kinetic Energy (KE) is the energy of motion. Potential energy is highest at the tops of hills right before the roller roaster rolls downward due to gravity. Kinetic energy is highest in the valleys, or lowest points, of the roller coaster because the roller coaster is speeding along quickly in these areas.

Potential and Kinetic Energy combine to make **Total Mechanical Energy** (TME). Total Mechanical Energy is the total amount of energy that is present during the entire rollercoaster ride. It's important to understand Total Mechanical Energy because it fits with the Law of Conservation of Energy which states that energy can neither be created nor destroyed. It can only be converted to a different form. In this case, energy goes from being potential energy to kinetic energy during different parts of the ride.

1. What is Potential Energy?
   - **A.** Energy of motion
   - **B.** Energy of change
   - **C.** Energy of position
   - **D.** Stored energy

2. What is Kinetic Energy?
   - **A.** Energy of motion
   - **B.** Energy of change
   - **C.** Energy of position
   - **D.** Stored energy

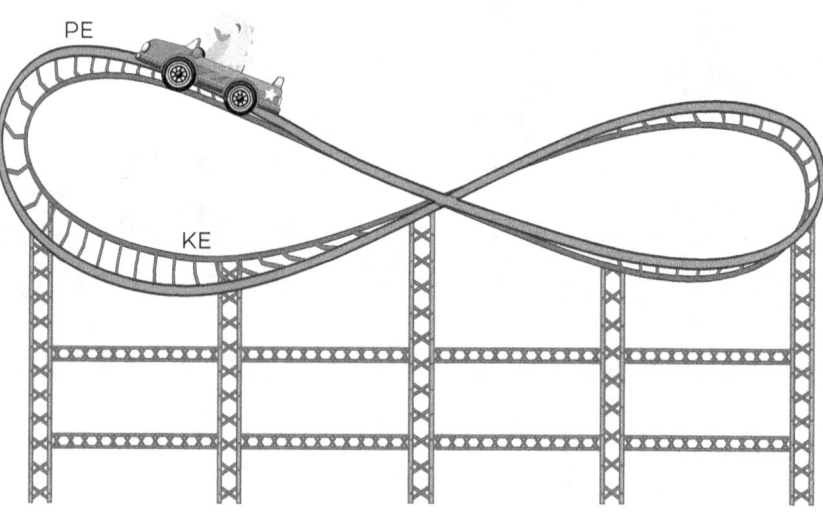

3. What is Total Mechanical Energy?

   A. Kinetic Energy + Potential Energy

   B. Kinetic Energy - Potential Energy

   C. Potential Energy - Kinetic Energy

   D. Potential Energy × Kinetic Energy

4. The Law of Conservation of Energy states that:

   A. Energy is lost over time.

   B. Energy is created and destroyed.

   C. Energy can't be created but can be destroyed.

   D. Energy can't be created or destroyed.

Yesterday you learned about the energy of motion! Today let's explore it in action with some activities.

Directions: Try out the tests below and answer the questions about your observations.

Test 1 - Ball Drop

Materials:

1. Tennis Ball

Procedure:

1. Hold a tennis ball head-high. (At this moment, it has maximum PE).
2. Drop the tennis ball. (At the exact moment it hits the ground, it has maximum KE).
3. Watch what happens!

Follow-Up Questions:

1. What happens to the ball after it hits the ground and bounces back up? Do you think it has more Potential Energy or more Kinetic Energy?

    A. More KE as it goes back up

    B. More PE as it goes back up

    C. Less PE as it goes back up

    D. It gains KE as it goes back up

2. Once the ball hits the ground and bounces back up again, are each of the following bounces as high as the first? Why or why not?

Test 2 - Changes in Potential Energy

Using the same tennis ball from the previous test, hold the ball at hip height and drop it. Watch what happens.

Follow-Up Questions:

3. Did the tennis ball bounce higher, lower or the same height as it did in the first test?

   A. Higher

   B. Lower

   C. Same height

   D. The ball did not bounce

4. At what point do you think the KE was highest in this test?

   A. When the ball was at hip height

   B. As the ball was falling

   C. When the ball hit the ground

   D. After the ball hit the ground and started moving back up into the air

Yesterday you explored potential and kinetic energy using a tennis ball. Today you will explain what you observed and relate it back to the Law of Conservation of Energy.

Directions: Read and answer the questions below.

1. Did the ball have more potential energy when it was held at head height or at hip height?

   A. Head

   B. Hip

2. What part of a rollercoaster could the tennis ball represent?

   A. The breaks

   B. The car

   C. The tallest hill

   D. The track itself

3. Remember the Law of Conservation of Energy? If energy can neither be created nor destroyed, then where did the energy go when you bounced the ball during test 1? It should have kept bouncing forever, right? Explain how the Law of Conservation of Energy applies to Kinetic and Potential Energy when you bounced the ball, and what happened to the energy that was lost.

You have discovered that the Law of Conservation of Energy means that once energy is applied to a system, it is not lost but rather changes into other forms. You have also discovered that Total Mechanical Energy is the sum of Kinetic Energy and Potential Energy, and that the balance shifts between the two depending on position. Today we are going to apply our knowledge by designing our own rollercoaster!

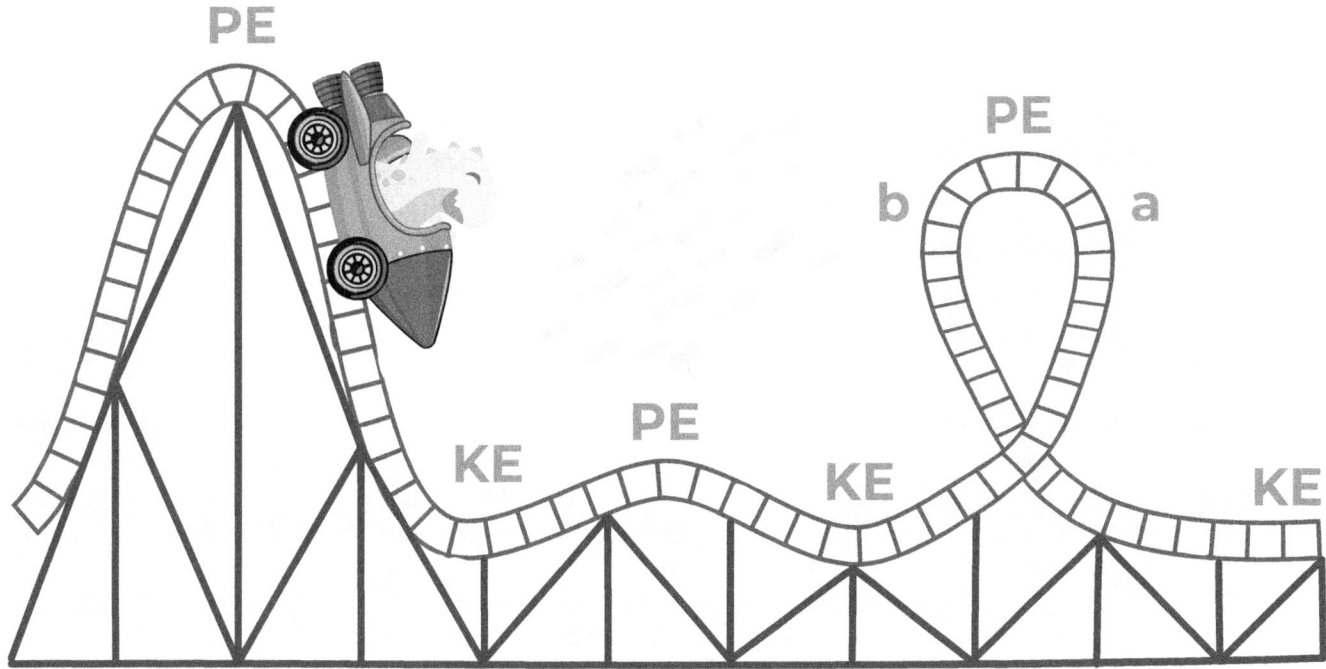

Follow-Up Questions:

1. Look at the image of the rollercoaster and notice the areas where PE and KE are labelled. In between those sections, PE and KE are mixed. For example, the last person in the roller coaster car going down the hill is going to have a higher PE and lower KE. The person in the front row of the roller coaster car has a higher KE and lower PE.

   A. With this information, look at the loop. At point "a" on the image: Do you think there will be a higher PE or higher KE? Circle one: Potential or Kinetic

   B. Look at the loop at point "b": Do you think there will be a higher PE or higher KE? Circle one: Potential or Kinetic

2. You work for an engineering company that has been tasked with designing a roller coaster for a new theme park. You have been reminded to design your roller coaster with the following in mind:

   A. Theme: Come up with an exciting story that will draw in crowds so they actually want to pay money to ride it!

   B. Budget: The budget for the roller coaster has to be realistic. Research other roller coasters so you know how much it will cost to build yours.

   C. Safety: What kinds of safety measures will you be adding to your coaster to make sure riders have an enjoyable ride every time?

   D. Physics: How will you design your roller coaster so it has only one mechanical element in the beginning and then continues moving on its own Kinetic and Potential Energy all the way to the end?

   E. Thrills: Your roller coaster must be exciting! There should be a big drop, at least one loop, a hill, and possibly some other elements in the middle to make the ride fun. Show where the Kinetic Energy and Potential Energy will be highest on your roller coaster similar to the image at the beginning of today's lesson.

3. Keeping all of the specifications in mind, write your plans out and draw your roller coaster. It is okay to make multiple drafts until you come up with one that you really like. Look back at the checklist to make sure you covered everything. You will need to write some things and draw some things for your final report to the theme park executives. Have fun with it!

4. Extension: Go ahead to Weeks 16 - 20, Engineering, to build a prototype model of your roller coaster!

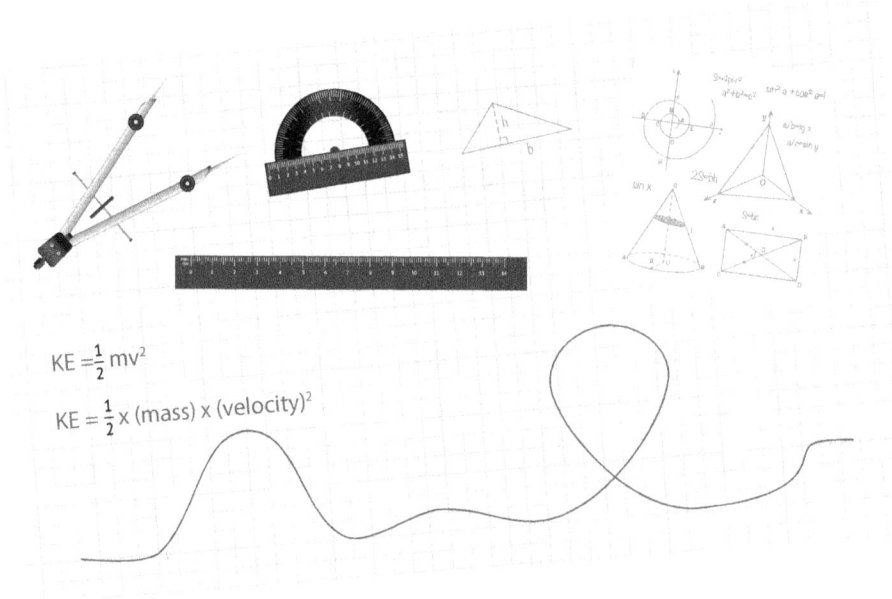

$$KE = \frac{1}{2} mv^2$$

$$KE = \frac{1}{2} \times (\text{mass}) \times (\text{velocity})^2$$

Today you will put together everything you have discovered this week about Kinetic and Potential Energy and elaborate on how they are connected in both real world applications as well as your roller coaster design from day 4.

Directions: Read and answer each question below.

1. If a car is traveling to the top of a hill and stops at the top, the energy of the engine changes to what other type of energy?

2. If energy can neither be created nor destroyed, where does the energy for the car's engine come from?
   Hint: think about what powers your car.

3. Why do you think it is important to design a roller coaster so that the ride begins with a very large hill?

....

....

....

4. If you add up the PE and the KE of all the different parts of your roller coaster, what will you have? What does it represent?

....

....

....

5. Did you have fun designing your own roller coaster this week?

   A. Yes

   B. No

WEEK 3

Physical Science

Energy: Thermodynamics

MS-PS3-3

Solid   Liquid   Gas

Apply scientific principles to design, construct, and test a device that either minimizes or maximizes thermal energy transfer.

Directions: Read the text below. Then answer the questions that follow.

What is Thermodynamics?

Thermodynamics sounds like a really big fancy word, but it is just a term that scientists use to describe the movement of energy from one location to another in objects. This energy movement is tracked through **heat transfer**. When objects lose or gain heat, the tiny particles that make them up, known as **atoms**, move slower or faster. Heat moves from areas of higher energy to lower energy because of temperature differences. For example, if you touched a cold rock on the ground, heat from your finger would be transferred to the cold rock. The energy in the atoms of your hand was higher, so it moved to the lower energy of the rock. This movement would happen until the atoms in both objects reached **equilibrium** or were the same level of energy.

This energy transfer relates to the **First Law of Thermodynamics**, also known as the **Law of Conservation of Energy** which states that energy can neither be created nor destroyed, only changed. You learned about this last week in your lessons about energy. In the previous example, heat from your hand was not destroyed, it simply moved to another object. Heat was not created in the rock, it was gained from your hand.

1. Thermodynamics can simply be described as

   A. A fancy word that physicists use to make themselves sound smart
   B. Heat gain
   C. Changing from one state of matter to another
   D. Movement of energy from one location to another in objects

2. Heat moves from

   A. Lower to higher heat energy
   B. One equal heat energy to another
   C. Higher to lower heat energy
   D. Heat doesn't move

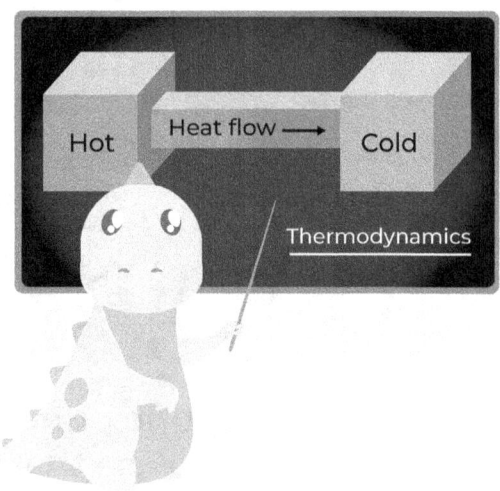

3. Equilibrium means having

   A. The same temperature
   B. Higher temperature
   C. Lower temperature
   D. Different temperatures

Yesterday you learned about heat transfer in thermodynamics. Today you will explore this phenomenon through various demonstrations.

Directions: Complete the following activities and answer the questions that follow.

A. Hold an ice cube in your hand and wait a few moments until it begins to melt.

1. How does the ice cube feel in your hand?

2. What is causing the ice cube to melt?

   A. The loss of heat from your hand to the ice cube

   B. The destruction of heat in the ice cube

   C. The creation of heat in the ice cube

   D. The equilibrium of energy in both your hand and the ice cube

B. Place a piece of bread in a toaster and toast it for a couple minutes. Afterwards, spread some butter on it and enjoy this tasty snack!

3. What object in this activity has the highest energy?

    A. The bread

    B. The toaster

    C. The knife

    D. The butter

4. What caused the butter to melt on the toast?

Yesterday you explored how heat transfer can occur between objects of different temperatures. Today you will explain how this relates to thermodynamics.

In the first activity, you learned that the energy in your hand was high and the heat of your hand transferred to the ice cube, causing it to melt.

1. The ice cube went from being a .... to being a ....

   A. gas/ solid

   B. solid/ gas

   C. liquid/ solid

   D. solid/ liquid

2. From this demonstration, you can see that .... in the form of .... can cause matter to change states, such as changing a liquid to a gas.

   A. atoms/ heat

   B. energy/ heat

   C. heat/ liquids

   D. energy/ electricity

In the second activity, you learned there was a transfer of heat from the toaster to the bread that caused the bread to toast. There was also a transfer of heat from the bread to the butter that caused the butter to melt.

3. If the toast and the butter were in equilibrium, what would that mean?

4. Could there be a transfer of heat from room temperature bread to the toaster? Why or why not?

Energy: Thermodynamics

EXPERIMENTING WITH THE TOPIC

Yesterday you explained how heat and energy transfer occurs in everyday objects. Today you will do an experiment where you will see the differences between the movement of molecules in different temperatures of water.

Background: When matter heats up, it begins to circulate in a current known as a **convection current**. A convection current is where warm air or liquids rise up and then cool and sink back down again, creating a continuous circular motion. The heat in your home behaves this way, as does the magma circulating under the Earth's crust.

Materials:

1. Two clear glasses or beakers
2. Almost boiling hot water
3. Ice water
4. Food coloring (one color)

Procedure:

1. Carefully pour the very hot water in one glass.
2. Pour the ice water in the other glass, being careful not to get any ice in the glass at all.
3. Put 5 drops of food coloring into each glass.

Follow-Up Questions:

1. How does the food coloring respond in the hot water when you first drop it in versus in the cold water?

....

....

....

....

2. After a couple of minutes, how does the food coloring behave in the two temperatures of water?

....

....

....

....

3. Does the food coloring stay near the bottom in the cold water?

   A. Yes

   B. No

4. Do you notice a circular movement of the food color/ water?

   A. Yes

   B. No

Yesterday you experimented with different temperatures of water in order to model convection currents. Today you will elaborate on how they relate to thermodynamics and the transfer of heat.

Directions: Read and think about each of the questions below and answer in complete sentences.

1. Which glass of water had more energy at the beginning of the experiment?
   A. The glass of cold water
   B. The glass of hot water
   C. They were in equilibrium

2. Why did you add food coloring to the water?

   ....

   ....

   ....

   ....

3. If you left the glasses of water alone for a few hours, what would happen to the food coloring in both of them?

   ....

   ....

   ....

   ....

4. Inference: Convection currents show you that the energy in warmer water causes the .... in the water to move ....
   A. energy/ slowly
   B. atoms/ quickly
   C. Food coloring/ downward
   D. equilibrium/ slowly

WEEK 4

Physical Science

Energy of Molecules

MS-PS1-4

Develop a model that predicts and describes changes in particle motion, temperature, and state of a pure substance when thermal energy is added or removed.

ARGOPREP

Directions: Read the text below. Then answer the questions that follow.

Molecules Matter

Kinetic energy is the energy of motion. But did you know this motion is not just present in visible objects? It also occurs on a much smaller scale. Even the tiny particles that make up the water in a glass or the air moving around your room are in constant motion. Surfaces that appear solid and stationary to our eyes are always moving too! These tiny particles are the **atoms** and **molecules** that make up objects, and they move faster or slower depending on the state and temperature of the matter.

In solid objects, molecules move very slowly and are positioned close together in an orderly fashion with only a small amount of kinetic energy. In liquids, the molecules have more kinetic energy than solids because they are positioned farther apart and are moving around more freely. In gases, there is no structure to the molecules, and kinetic energy is high because movement between molecules is random. The molecules are able to move freely and collide with each other within the space. As temperature increases, kinetic energy also increases. This means the hotter matter gets, the more randomly and erratically its molecules move around. As these molecules begin to move faster, they spread out because they need more space to accommodate the extra movement. This leads us to the **Kinetic Theory of Matter**, or the idea that all matter is made of atoms and molecules that are constantly moving, and when heat is added, kinetic energy increases.

1. Which type of matter has the most kinetic energy?

   A. Solid

   B. Liquid

   C. Gas

   D. Molecules

2. Which type of matter has the most order to its molecules?

   A. Solid

   B. Liquid

   C. Gas

   D. Kinetic

3. Restate the Kinetic Theory of Matter.

Yesterday you learned about the Kinetic Theory of Matter. Today you will explore this theory by drawing models that represent the molecules in different types of matter.

Background: Since the kinetic energy of molecules in an object changes depending on the object's temperature, we can assume that as the state of matter changes from a solid to a liquid to a gas, the matter also gets warmer. As matter changes from a gas to a liquid to a solid it gets colder. This goes for any material. By changing temperature, or forcing kinetic energy to slow down, we can convert a gas like nitrogen to a liquid. Liquid nitrogen is used in the medical field.

Directions: Using the boxes below, draw molecules of an object when it is a solid, liquid, and a gas. Draw all your molecules as circles and add arrows to show the movement or direction of the molecules. If molecules are moving fast, you can draw more arrows in a row (-> -> ->). If the molecules are moving slow, you can draw only one arrow (->).

Picturing Moving Molecules

Solid   **Liquid**   **Gas**

Yesterday you drew models of the movement of molecules in different states of matter in order to represent the kinetic theory of motion. Today you will explain how your models can help you think about matter all around you.

Directions: Answer the questions that follow.

1. Think about the drawing you did for a gas. If you added more heat to those molecules, what would happen? How would you represent this in a drawn model?

2. Which state of matter had the fewest arrows in your drawing? Why?

3. Let's pretend the molecules you drew in your model of a liquid represented water. Could water molecules also be found in a model of a gas or a solid? What do we call these forms of water?

4. In which of your drawings did you draw the molecules closest together? Why don't these molecules need as much space around them?

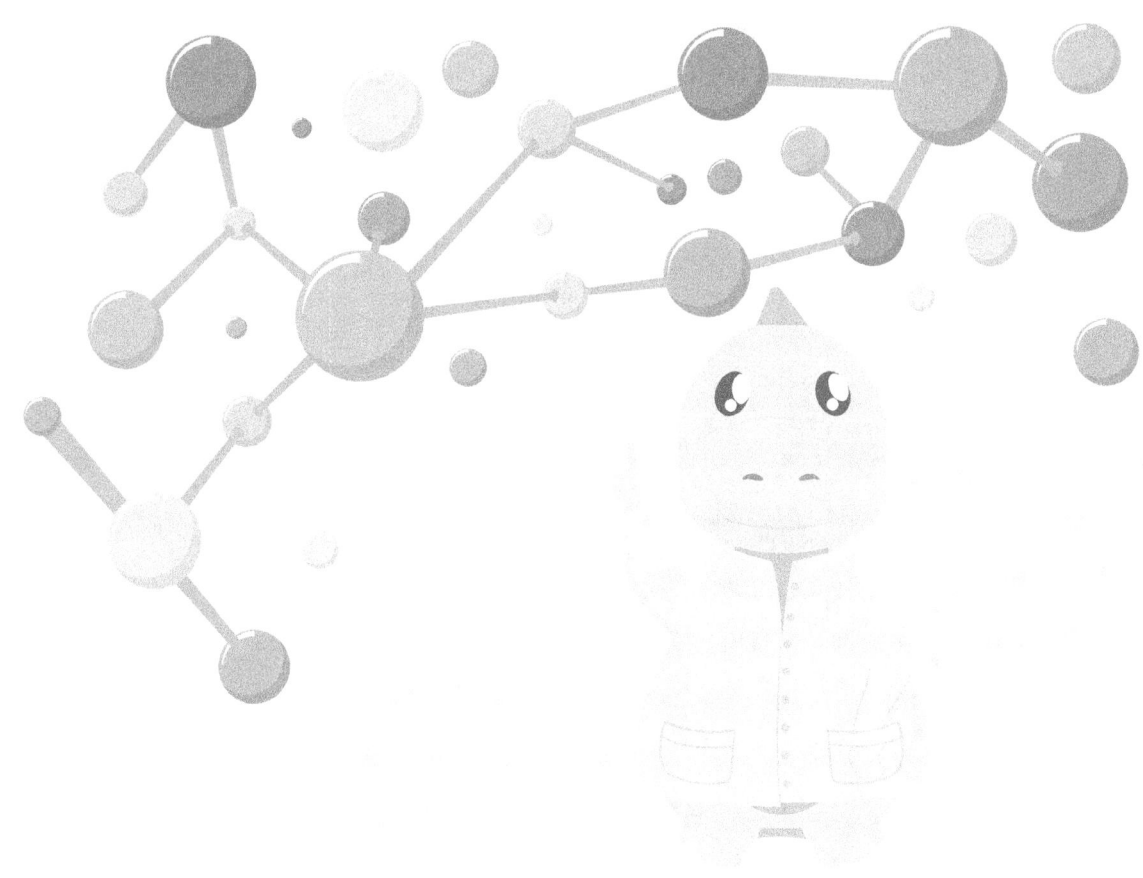

Yesterday you explained how your drawn models of molecules related to the kinetic theory of motion. Today you will be doing an experiment to see the thermal expansion of air. You will be using a balloon to help witness the expansion and contraction of air molecules as the temperature rises and falls.

Materials:

1. 2 Balloons
2. Bowl of hot water
3. Bowl of ice water
4. Ruler
5. String or yarn

Procedure:

1. Blow up your first balloon and tie it.
2. Measure your balloon's diameter from side to side and record it here: _____ cm
3. Place your balloon over the bowl of ice water for 5 minutes.
4. Measure your balloon's diameter from side to side and record it here: _____ cm
5. Blow up your second balloon and tie it.
6. Measure your balloon's diameter from side to side and record it here: _____ cm
7. Place your balloon over the bowl of hot water for 5 minutes.
8. Measure your balloon's diameter from side to side and record it here: _____ cm

Results:

1. Calculate the decrease of the ice water balloon 1 by subtracting the resulting diameter from the initial diameter: .... cm.

2. Calculate the growth of the hot water balloon 2 by subtracting the resulting diameter from the initial diameter: .... cm.

3. Which balloon grew more?

....

....

Yesterday you experimented with the concept of how temperature can change gas trapped in a balloon. Today you will explain how this relates back to the main focus of the week, the Kinetic Theory of Motion.

Directions: Read and think about each of the questions below, and answer in complete sentences.

1. In yesterday's experiment, what happened to the air molecules inside of the balloon when the temperature was decreased?

2. What happened to the air molecules inside of the balloon when the temperature was increased?

3. Think about a hot air balloon. A hot flame is used under the balloon to heat up the air inside of the balloon. What does this do to the hot air balloon?

4. What do you think would happen if you continued to drop the temperature of the balloon in this experiment?

WEEK 5

Physical Science

Wave Energy in Technology

MS-PS4-1

Use mathematical representations to describe a simple model for waves that includes how the amplitude of a wave is related to the energy in a wave.

ARGOPREP

Directions: Read the text below. Then answer the questions that follow.

Catch a Wave

You may know of ocean waves, but there are many other kinds of waves too. Have you ever gotten a sunburn? Used a microwave to cook food? Received an x-ray at the hospital? We come into contact with **waves** every day but don't even realize the impact they have on our lives. Luckily, scientists and engineers do! They study the properties of different kinds of waves in order to find ways to use them to make our lives better. The technology produced from studying waves has been put into everyday objects like sunglasses, radios, speakers, medical equipment, weather prediction, microwave ovens, cell phones, and more. By understanding different kinds of waves, engineers ensure that your cell phone call connects to only the person you are calling and not everyone making a call at the same time. Waves let you tune in to the right radio station and the correct walkie talkie channel. Even sunlight comes in the form of wave energy entering our atmosphere from outer space.

1. Using the internet, look up the scientific name for four different wave types. Some were mentioned in the above reading, but see if you can find some new ones as well!

   A.

   B.

   C.

   D.

2. Why do engineers study the properties of different waves? More than one answer is correct.

   A. To keep busy at their jobs   **C.** To go surfing

   B. To protect us   **D.** To develop new technologies

3. Give one example of a technology or a product that has been developed thanks to our scientific understanding of UV rays, a type of light wave.

Yesterday you learned about waves and how our understanding of them is used every day. Today you will calculate how waves can travel fast and slow, just like the molecules we discussed last week when you learned about the Kinetic Theory of Motion.

Directions: Read the text below. Then answer the questions that follow.

So far, we have discussed energy in terms of matter and the movement of atoms and molecules. However, when we talk about waves, we are talking about the movement of pure energy. Depending on the kind of wave, this energy moves either faster or slower. One way that we measure a wave is by its **wavelength**. Wavelength is the distance between a specific point on two waves that are next to each other. This is usually the crest of the wave (top), but it can be the trough (bottom) or some other point as long as it's the same point for both. Wavelength is usually measured in meters.

Wave frequency is the number of waves that pass a specific point in a certain amount of time. Think about it this way! If you were sitting on a surfboard in the ocean, the number of waves that passed under you in 60 seconds would be the wave frequency. You could compare wave frequency by going to your favorite spot on a calm day and counting the waves in 60 seconds versus the number of waves that would pass under you when you went to that same spot on a rough day. Wave frequency is measured in Hertz (Hz); 1 Hertz = 1 wave/second. Wavelength and wave frequency are inversely proportional. This means that as one goes up, the other goes down. Here are two equations to show the relationship between wave speed, wavelength, and wave frequency:

$$\text{Wave Speed} = \text{Wavelength} \times \text{Wave Frequency}$$

$$\text{Wave Frequency} = \frac{\text{Wave Speed}}{\text{Wavelength}}$$

How fast or slow a wave moves is called its wave speed. Wave speed is the distance a wave travels in a specific amount of time and is measured in meters/second. For example, if you measured a wave that moved 6000 meters in 60 seconds, you know that the wave speed is 100 meters/second. We can calculate wave speed like this:

$$\text{Wave Speed} = \frac{\text{Distance}}{\text{Time}}$$

Follow-Up Questions:

1. An ocean wave from trough to trough measures a distance of 3 meters long. It takes 1.5 seconds for the wave to pass by the post of a pier. What is the wave speed of the ocean wave?

2. Julia makes waves by moving a Slinky back and forth. The wavelength is 0.2 meters and the wave frequency is 3 Hertz. What is the wave speed of the Slinky?

3. Jesse sings a note with a frequency of 275 Hz. When singing in the living room, the note has a wave speed of 340 m/s. However, when singing outside on a hot sunny day the wave speed of the note is 350 m/s. What is the difference in wavelength when singing inside versus outside?

4. A tsunami has been triggered by an undersea earthquake and is traveling across the open ocean at a speed of 200 m/s (about 500 mph). The wavelength tracked by satellite is 500 km (about 300 miles). Quickly calculate the wave frequency of the incoming tsunami so you can warn everyone within its collision radius! Make sure you use the same units of measurement in your calculations.

Yesterday you explored the relationships between wavelength, wave speed and wave frequency. Today you will explain how these three measurements of waves might look or how you can demonstrate them.

Directions: Read the directions for each demo. Then answer the questions that follow.

Take a long rope (about 5 ft) and tie one side to a chair. Hold the other end in your hand and move your arm up and down once every two seconds.

1. What do you notice is created in the shape of the movement in the rope when you whip your hand up and down?

2. What is the wave frequency?

Now, using that same rope, move your arm up and down once every second.

3. What did you change by moving your arm more rapidly? There is more than one correct answer.

Now take the rope and cut off 1 ft of its length. Tie it back onto the chair and create a wave every two seconds by moving your arm up and down.

4. By cutting the rope, what wave measurement did you change? There is more than one correct answer.

Yesterday you explained how wave measurements relate to the movement of a rope. Today you will do a basic experiment to see how sound waves move. Sound waves, like light waves, are waves we can't see unless we have help. In this case, we'll use a tissue!

Background: Like light, sound moves in waves. Very low tones are made up of waves that move slowly with a low frequency. Higher pitched sounds are made up of waves that have a quick wave speed and higher frequency. This means when you go to a concert, you are listening to music that is made up of lots of different sound waves with different wave speeds, wave frequencies and wavelengths.

Materials:

1. Tissue
2. Speaker
3. Music
4. Tape

Procedure:

1. Tape just the top edge of a tissue onto a speaker so that it is hanging down in front of it.
2. Play different kinds of music out of the speaker.

Follow-Up Questions:

1. What happened to the tissue when you played music out of the speaker?

....

....

2. Why did the tissue change its movements as the music changed?

....

....

3. Do you think you could figure out either wave speed, wavelength, or wave frequency by watching the tissue? Explain.

....

....

....

Yesterday you experimented with sound waves. Today you will elaborate on your observations and connect them back to the idea of waves.

Directions: Read and think about each of the questions below, and answer in complete sentences.

1. In order to visualize sound waves, we needed to place a tissue on the speaker. How else could you determine information about sound waves? Hint: play some music and put your hand on the speaker.

....

....

....

2. If you wanted to measure the frequency of one of the soundwaves you heard, what two pieces of information would you need?

....

....

....

3. Look at the image of the Electromagnetic Spectrum on page 53. As you can see from the wave illustration at the top, moving from left to right, the wavelength becomes shorter. Therefore, as you move from left to right, the frequency increases. These changes relate to energy.

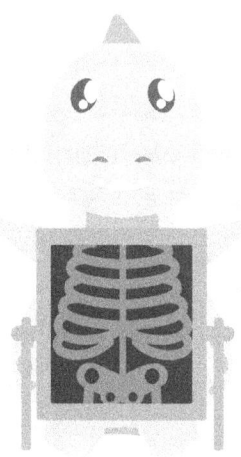

Week 5 Day 5

Wave Energy in Technology

ELABORATING ON THE TOPIC

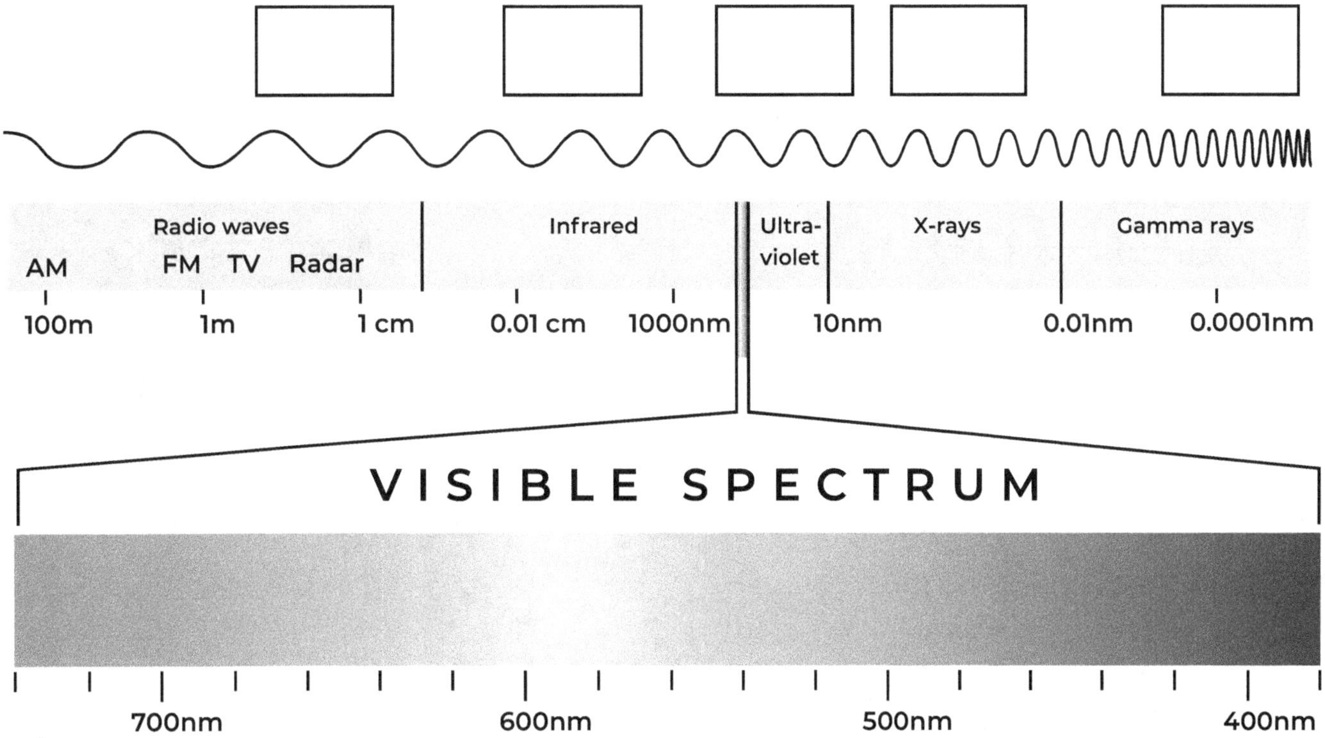

Radio waves
AM
FM
TV
Radar
Infrared
Ultra-violet
X-rays
Gamma rays
100m
1m
1 cm
0.01 cm
1000nm
10nm
0.01nm
0.0001nm
VISIBLE SPECTRUM
700nm
600nm
500nm
400nm

A. According to the diagram above, which would have higher energy, x-rays or TV waves?

....

B. According to this diagram, do sound waves or light waves move faster?

....

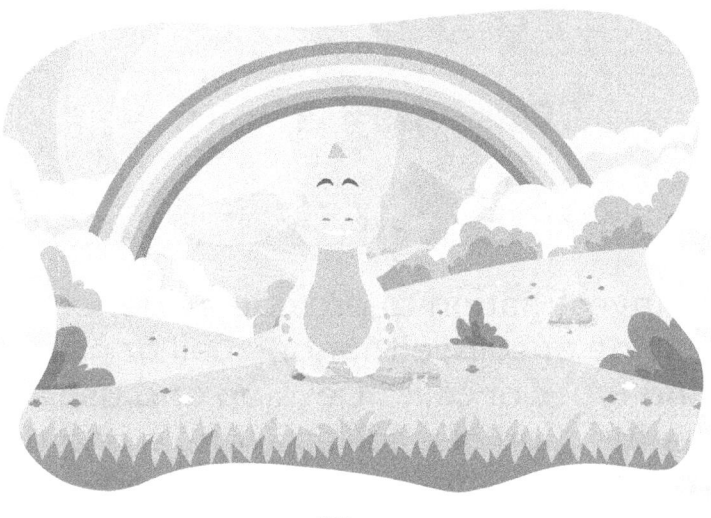

Life Science
Cell Theory

MS-LS1-1&2

Conduct an investigation to provide evidence that living things are made of cells; either one cell or many different numbers and types of cells. Develop and use a model to describe the function of a cell as a whole and the ways that parts of cells contribute to its function.

Directions: Read the text below. Then answer the questions that follow.

What is The Cell Theory?

Prepare to have your mind blown! All living things are made out of **cells**...it's true! Cells are the tiniest parts of any living thing - think of them like the building blocks of life. You, me, your dog or cat, the tree your piece of paper came from, even the bacteria crawling on your skin right now are all made up of cells. Some organisms are **unicellular**, meaning they are very tiny and are only made up of one single cell. Other organisms are multicellular, meaning they are made of many cells stuck together. This is what you are, a **multicellular** organism. No matter what kind of organism they are, all living things follow specific rules that make up **The Cell Theory**:

A. All living things are made of cells.

B. Cells divide to make new cells.

C. Cells are the smallest part of an organism.

But what do these rules mean? Let's take them apart so that we can understand them better. The first rule, "All living things are made of cells" is pretty self explanatory, but to understand it fully, we need to know what a living thing is. Living things have specific characteristics that set them apart from nonliving things. All living things:

* Have One or More Cells
* Reproduce
* Eat Food
* Control their Internal Environment
* Pass on Genes
* Respond to Outside Stimuli
* Grow
* Adapt

The second rule, "Cells divide to make new cells" tells us that cells cannot simply appear out of nowhere. They must grow, divide, and in doing so, multiply. The final rule states: "Cells are the smallest part of an organism," meaning that cells are the smallest whole part of a living thing. There are, of course, smaller parts that make up a cell called organelles, but an organelle cannot survive on its own and produce other living creatures. Only a whole cell can do that.

1. What are the three parts of The Cell Theory?

    A.

    B.

    C.

2. What is the term for the parts that make up the cell?

    A. Molecules

    B. Organelles

    C. Preons

    D. Sub-atomic particles

3. True or False: All living things must have more than one cell in order to be considered "alive."

    A. True

    B. False

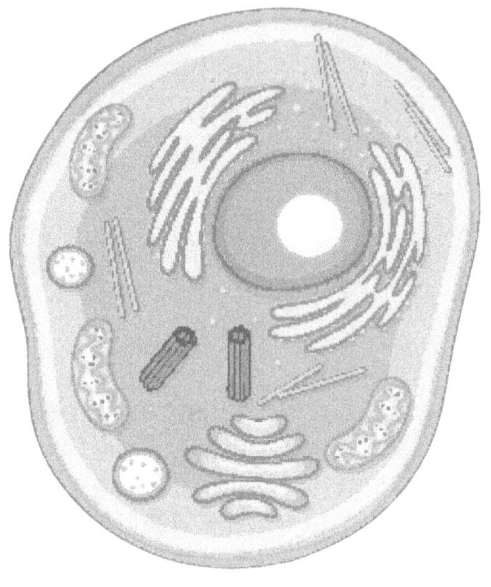

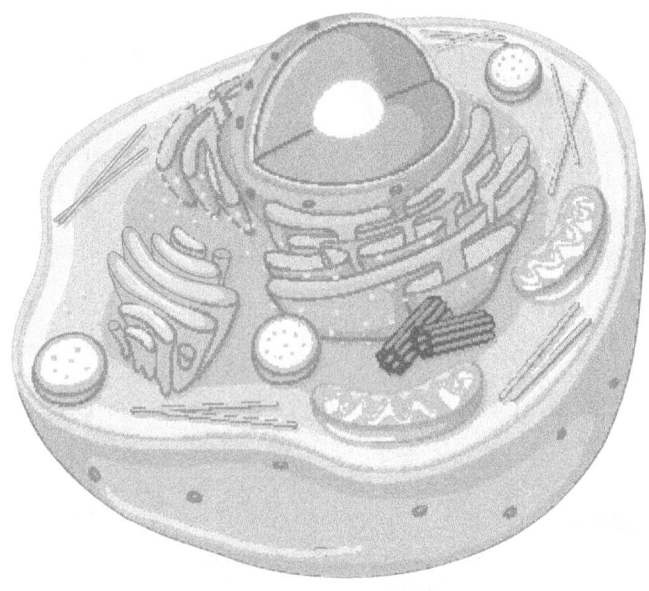

Yesterday you learned about cell theory and that all living things are made of cells. Today you will use what you discovered about The Cell Theory to create a song or poem to help you remember the three rules!

Directions: Read and answer the questions below.

A. The Cell Theory is an important concept in biology, so it's important to remember it. Using the three parts of The Cell Theory, you are going to write a song! Your song will be a great way for you to remember the three parts.

B. You might want to consider picking your favorite song and just re-writing the lyrics to that tune so that the new lyrics are all about The Cell Theory!

C. You can even take it a step farther and record your song or make a music video with a smartphone, iPad, or computer.

D. Make sure your song includes vocabulary like multicellular, unicellular and organelles.

E. Your song (or poem if you prefer) does not have to rhyme, but it may help you memorize the information better if it does.

Yesterday you wrote a catchy song or poem to help you remember the three main parts of The Cell Theory. Today you will learn more about the important organelles found in plant and animal cells.

Directions: Study the chart below on cell organelle structure and function by making flash cards. Then, fill out the Venn Diagram on the following page comparing and contrasting which organelles are found in plant cells, animal cells, or both kinds of cells.

Organelle Structure & Function

Name	Structure	Function	Plant/Animal
Nucleus	Has a membrane and a Nucleolus in the center; looks like an egg.	The "brain" of the cell; control center where DNA is located.	Both
Endoplasmic Reticulum	Two varieties, "rough" or "smooth;" a zig zagging tubelike structure located right next to the Nucleus.	Like a protein super highway for transporting mRNA and proteins from one part of the cell to another.	Both
Golgi Body	Looks like a stack of pancakes or a WiFi symbol.	The packing warehouse and shipping department of the cell. Protein is stored, packaged in vesicles, and shipped out of the cell.	Both
Mitochondria	Looks like a hot dog with mustard zig zagged on it.	The "powerhouse of the cell;" makes the energy for the cell through Cellular Respiration.	Both
Lysosome	A sac filled with digestive enzymes.	Patrols the cell getting rid of invaders by capturing them in the bubble, digesting them, and spitting them back outside of the cell.	Both
Ribosome	Tiny dots either free-floating in the cell or attached to the Rough Endoplasmic Reticulum.	The factory of the cell; they make the proteins using the directions from DNA that are translated by mRNA.	Both

Name	Structure	Function	Plant/Animal
Cytoplasm	All of the "empty" space in between the organelles.	The soup of the cell. A jelly-like substance that all of the organelles are suspended in.	Both
Plasma Membrane	The outermost part of an animal cell and the 2nd to outermost part of a plant cell just under the wide layer (Cell Wall).	A hydrophobic layer that is semipermeable. This means it repels water and allows some things in but keeps other things out.	Both
Vacuole	Pouch of liquid inside of the cell.	Like sports drink pouches, they contain water, salts, and sugar that are stored and used later when needed.	Animal
Centriole	Looks like rigatoni noodles.	Aids in cell division.	Animal
Central Vacuole	One giant pouch of liquid that takes up most of the space in a plant cell.	A giant pouch that contains water, salts, and sugar that is stored and used later when needed. Bigger than in animal cell because plants can't predict when they will get water next.	Plant
Chloroplast	Looks like an oval with tiny beans inside.	Contains chlorophyll and is responsible for photosynthesis inside of the plant cell.	Plant
Cell Wall	Outside of the plant cell.	Provides support and structure for the plant. Contains Lignin which helps plants stand up straight without falling over.	Plant

Fill out the Venn Diagram to compare and contrast the organelles that are found in only animal cells, only plant cells, or in both plant and animal cells.

Animal   **Both**   **Plant**

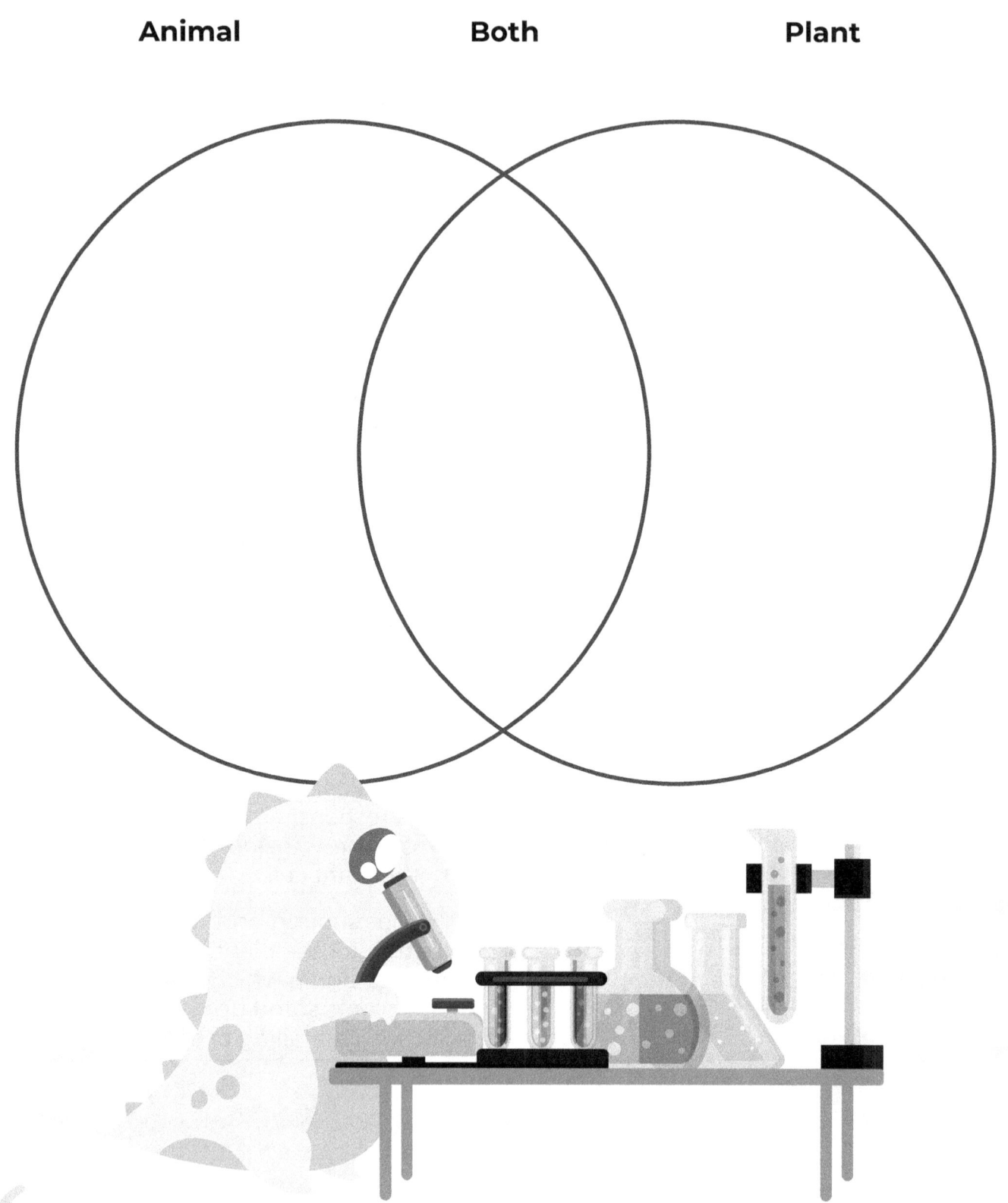

Yesterday you explained the similarities and differences between the organelles in plants and animals. Today you will put together what you have learned this week to make a 3D model of a cell complete with organelles.

Directions: You can choose to make a plant cell, animal cell, or both! Your cell can be made out of anything you want, but here are some ideas: PlayDoh, cake, recycled materials, styrofoam balls, clay, and/or paint. Your cell(s) must have organelles labeled, and the functions of each organelle must be written on a key (a paper that goes with your model). You can use the diagram from Day 2 for reference or other sources to help you.

Below, sketch out what your model will look like and label what you'll make each organelle out of.

Making a Cell

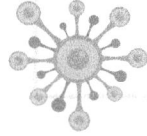

Yesterday you made a fun 3D model of a cell using the materials of your choosing. Today you will consider your Venn Diagram and your model so you can elaborate on your knowledge of cells and cell theory.

Directions: Consider everything you have discovered about cells this week, and answer the following questions in complete sentences.

1. Why do both plant and animal cells need a nucleus? How does this relate to The Cell Theory?

....

....

....

2. If a plant cell was missing its cell wall, would that be a bad thing? Why or why not?

....

....

....

3. Look at your hand and notice how it is made of skin cells. Where did those skin cells come from?

....

....

....

4. Can a single cell be considered an entire living organism?

....

....

....

WEEK 7

Life Science
Inheritance of Traits

MS-LS3-2

Develop and use a model to describe why asexual reproduction results in offspring with identical genetic information and sexual reproduction results in offspring with genetic variation.

Directions: : Read the text below. Then answer the questions that follow.

Genetics

Have you ever looked at your family members and thought about how alike you are? Maybe you have been told that you share certain characteristics with your relatives. **Characteristics** can be the way you look: your hair color, eye color, nose shape, height, or the shape of your ears. But characteristics can also be your mannerisms: your sense of humor, how good of a dancer you are, your math skill, your coordination, your facial expressions, even your musical inclination. So how does this happen? How are **genetic traits**, the characteristics coded into our DNA in the nucleus of all of our cells, passed on from one generation to the next?

Genetic traits have been passed to you from your biological parents. You have inherited a combination of **genes** passed to you from both your mother and your father. This week you will learn about how cells divide in order to copy their genes into new cells. Organisms can use these cells in their own bodies or pass the cells on to make a new organism called **offspring**.

1. A characteristic is best defined as:

   A. Things that make you the same as everyone else
   B. Things that make you different from everyone else
   C. The different traits that are passed on from one generation to the next
   D. Only the genetic traits that we can see

2. Where is DNA stored inside of the cell?

   A. Mitochondria
   B. Nucleus
   C. Ribosome
   D. Endoplasmic Reticulum

3. Where did your characteristics come from?

   A. Your mother
   B. Your father
   C. Your siblings
   D. Your mother and your father

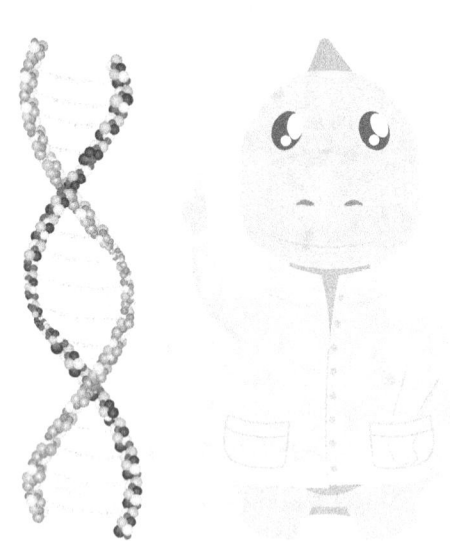

Yesterday you learned that your genetic traits are passed down from your biological parents. You also learned that genetic information is an important part of your cells. Today let's take a look at how cells divide to make more cells. This process is happening in your body right now!

Directions: Read each text below. Then answer the questions that follow.

What is Cellular Division?

Cells divide to make new cells all the time. It's easy to understand why this process is necessary to our survival. You might fall down and skin your knee, and after a few days, it seems like it is magically healed. How is this possible? Your body has the ability to make copies of skin cells so it can replace ones that have been damaged. This process happens even more frequently than you may think. In fact, your body loses about 40,000 skin cells every minute! Actually, most of the dust in your home is made up of old, dead skin cells.

Cell division is an important process because it makes sure the protective layer on your body keeps doing its job correctly. So how does this process work, and how long does it take for a cell to make a copy of itself? When a cell makes two identical copies of itself called **daughter cells**, it is known as **mitosis**. The daughter cells are known as **diploid** cells because they are identical copies of the original cell. They each contain a complete set of chromosomes. It takes about 24 hours for each new cell to grow and then go through mitosis. Mitosis is essential for the growth, repair, and maintenance of cells.

Let's take a look at a simplified diagram of what mitosis looks like during the different stages:

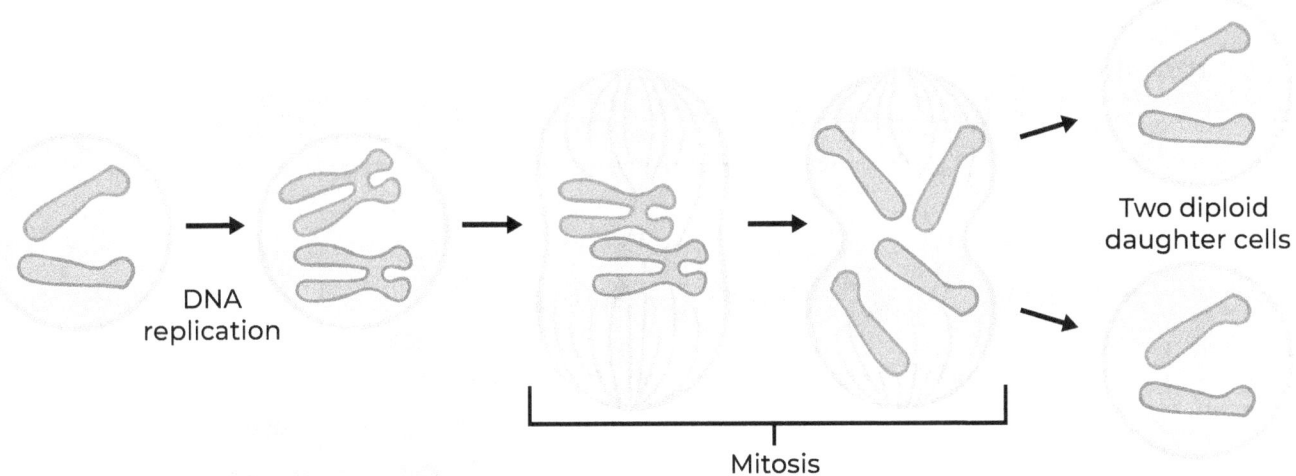

DNA replication

Mitosis

Two diploid daughter cells

There are 7 main players involved inside of a cell during mitosis. Here are their names, what they look like, and what their jobs are:

Organelles Involved in Mitosis

Organelle	Appearance	Function
Centriole	Shaped like rigatoni noodles.	Moves to opposite poles during Mitosis to deploy and reel in Spindle Fibers.
Nuclear Membrane	The outer covering of the Nucleus.	Protects the Nucleus and its contents.
Nucleus	Looks like the yolk of an egg.	Where DNA is located.
Spindle Fibers	Like fishing line that stretches across the cell from Centriole to Centriole.	Helps to pull the Sister Chromatids apart.
DNA	Looks like a spiral staircase or twisted ladder.	Contains all of the instructions that make every living creature unique.
Chromosomes	Made of one long strand of DNA wound up and stuck together with Protein glue.	Humans have 23 sets of paired chromosomes for a total of 46 chromosomes.
Sister Chromatids	Shaped like an X	Identical copies of chromosomes formed by DNA replication of a chromosome. The copies are joined together with a Centromere in the middle to form an X.

Now that you know who is involved in mitosis inside of a cell, let's look at the stages of mitosis and what happens during each stage inside of the cell:

Stages of Mitosis

Stage	What is happening	Process
Interphase		• The cell spends most of its time in this phase, growing, getting energy, and reading its DNA. • In late Interphase, the DNA is copied so that each chromosome will have a sister chromatid.
Prophase		• Chromosomes become visible in the Nucleus. • Centrioles move to opposite poles of the cell • Spindle Fibers start to form from the Centrioles. • Nuclear membrane breaks apart
Metaphase		• The sister chromatids line up in the middle of the cell • Spindle Fibers attach to the centromeres in the middle of each sister chromatid

Stage	What is happening	Process
Anaphase		• Sister chromatids are pulled apart into separate Chromosomes by the Spindle Fibers • Two genetically identical groups of Chromosomes are pulled toward opposite poles by Centrioles
Telophase		• Nuclear membranes form around the two sets of Chromosomes • Chromosomes start to spread out and unclump inside the nucleus • Spindle Fibers break down
Cytokinesis		• Cell splits apart into two daughter cells with same number of chromosomes as parent cell • In humans = two copies of 23 chromosomes • Diploid cells

Yesterday you learned about the process of mitosis and how different organelles help during its different stages. Today you will explain how mitosis works in a bit more detail.

Directions: Using the information you discovered yesterday, answer the following questions:

1. The process of dividing a cell to make two identical new daughter cells is known as ....

2. How long does it take for a new human skin cell to grow and then finish a complete cycle of mitosis?

   A. 5 minutes   **C.** 1 year

   B. 5 hours   **D.** 24 hours

3. Mitosis is important for what three things in living organisms?

4. How many skin cells does your body lose per minute?

   A. 4   **C.** 40,000

   B. 400   **D.** 4,000,000

5. List the steps of Mitosis in order:

   A.

   B.

   C.

   D.

   E.

   F.

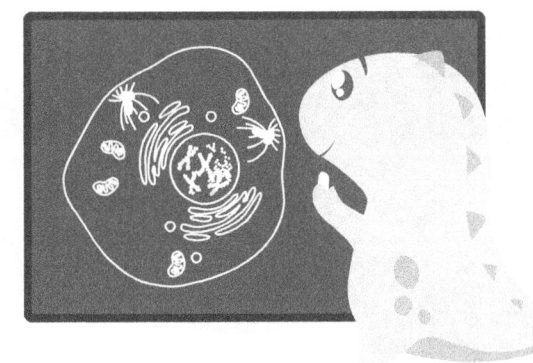

Yesterday you reinforced what you understood about the process of mitosis and why it is important. Today you will complete an exciting lab and look at pictures of cells undergoing mitosis that were taken with a microscope.

Materials:

1. 6 different colored pencils
2. pencil

Procedure:

1. The image below is of cells from a Broad Bean plant taken from a vertical cut through the tip of the root and put on a slide under a microscope. (Image courtesy of microscopy-uk.org.uk)
2. If you look closely at the cells in the image, you can see the cells are all undergoing different stages of mitosis. This is true in your body, too. Right now, your cells are dividing through all the different stages of mitosis. This is also how your body grows.
3. During this lab, you are going to be identifying, labeling, and drawing different cells at different stages in mitosis.

Follow-Up Questions:

1. Make a Key using your 6 colored pencils by coloring in the boxes with a different color next to each phase. Then outline the cells in the picture with the appropriate color.

   A. Interphase ☐

   B. Prophase ☐

   C. Metaphase ☐

   D. Anaphase ☐

   E. Telophase ☐

   F. Cytokinesis ☐

2. Which stage appears the most?

....

....

....

....

3. Do the cells under the microscope undergoing mitosis look the same as how you imagined they would? Why or why not?

....

....

....

....

....

....

Yesterday you analyzed actual images of cells in a Broad Bean plant and saw mitosis in action! Today you will pull together everything you have learned about mitosis and cellular division to draw conclusions about how they relate to the bigger picture for life.

Directions: Read and answer each question below.

1. Explain the connection between mitosis and the possibility of infants becoming full grown adults who carry a combination of their mother's and father's genetic traits.

_____

_____

_____

_____

_____

2. If a full cycle of Mitosis takes 24 hours to complete, why did the plant have cells going through all of the different stages of mitosis at once? What are the benefits of having every stage happening at a different time?

_____

_____

_____

_____

3. Extra Research: Find out how your body heals a scraped knee, and provide a summary. How does mitosis help with the process?

_____

_____

_____

_____

WEEK 8

Life Science

Energy Flow through Organisms

MS-LS1-6

Construct a scientific explanation based on evidence for the role of photosynthesis in the cycling of matter and flow of energy into and out of organisms.

ARGOPREP

Directions: Read the text below. Then answer the questions that follow.

What is an Ecosystem?

Have you ever considered where your food comes from? Think about it for a moment. What was the last meal you ate? Chances are that meal came from a grocery store, or maybe some of it came from your own garden or a community-supported agriculture, such as a farm. If we try and trace your meal all the way back to its origins, most of it would come from a farm. But what about the rest of the animal kingdom? When they need something to eat, they don't have the luxury of heading down to their local store to pick up some food. So how do they find what they need to ensure their survival?

Different animals live in specific **ecosystems** or areas of land that have certain abiotic and biotic conditions that meet their needs. **Abiotic** conditions are the nonliving parts of an ecosystem like temperature, air, water, sunlight, wind, rocks, space, and water. **Biotic** conditions are the living parts of an ecosystem like other animals, plants, trees, sticks, log debris in a stream, leaf litter, and bugs. Living organisms have five basic needs for survival: food, water, air, shelter, and other members of their species. It is important that an ecosystem meets these five basic needs equally in order for an organism to survive there. This week we are focusing on food since it is where an organism gets its energy.

1. What is an Ecosystem?

    A. An area of land that has poor living conditions

    B. Where you live

    C. An area of land that meets basic needs

    D. The whole Earth

2. Which of the following are some examples of abiotic conditions?

    A. Dirt, worms, sunlight

    B. Leaves, rocks, sticks

    C. Water, soil, cardinal

    D. Temperature, wind, hills

3. Which of the following is not a basic need for survival?

    A. Water

    B. Entertainment

    C. Food

    D. Shelter

Yesterday you learned about ecosystems and that living organisms need certain resources in order to survive. Today you will look more deeply into the resource of food and learn about food webs in an ecosystem.

Directions: Read the following passage and then answer the questions that follow.

> We can track the movement of energy from one organism to another in an ecosystem by using a **Food Web**. A food web tracks which organisms eat which other organisms in an ecosystem. All energy on Earth begins with plants. Plants are known as **Producers** because they get their energy from the sun. After the Producers, are the **Primary Consumers**, or the first organism that eats the plant. Primary Consumers can either be **Herbivores** (they only eat plants) or **Omnivores** (organisms that eat both plants and other animals). After Primary Consumers are **Secondary Consumers**. Secondary Consumers eat the Primary Consumers and can be either Omnivores or Carnivores (animals that eat only other animals). After Secondary Consumers are **Tertiary Consumers** and then **Quaternary Consumers**, which are usually Carnivores. At the highest level of a Food Web is the **Apex Predator**, which is an organism that is not eaten by any other organism. Examples of apex predators are Great White Sharks, Orcas, Tigers, Lions, Grizzly Bears, and Wolves.

1. What do producers make that consumers cannot make on their own?

2. Which of these is not usually a primary consumer?

   A. Producer

   B. Carnivore

   C. Secondary Consumer

   D. All of the above

3. A quaternary consumer could also be what?

   A. A plant

   B. An herbivore

   C. An apex predator

   D. A producer

Yesterday you found out food webs begin with a plant and follow a specific path from animal to animal. Today you will explore a real food web and answer questions about it.

Directions: Take a look at this Food Web from the Chesapeake Bay and answer the questions below.

Chesapeake Bay Waterbird Food Web

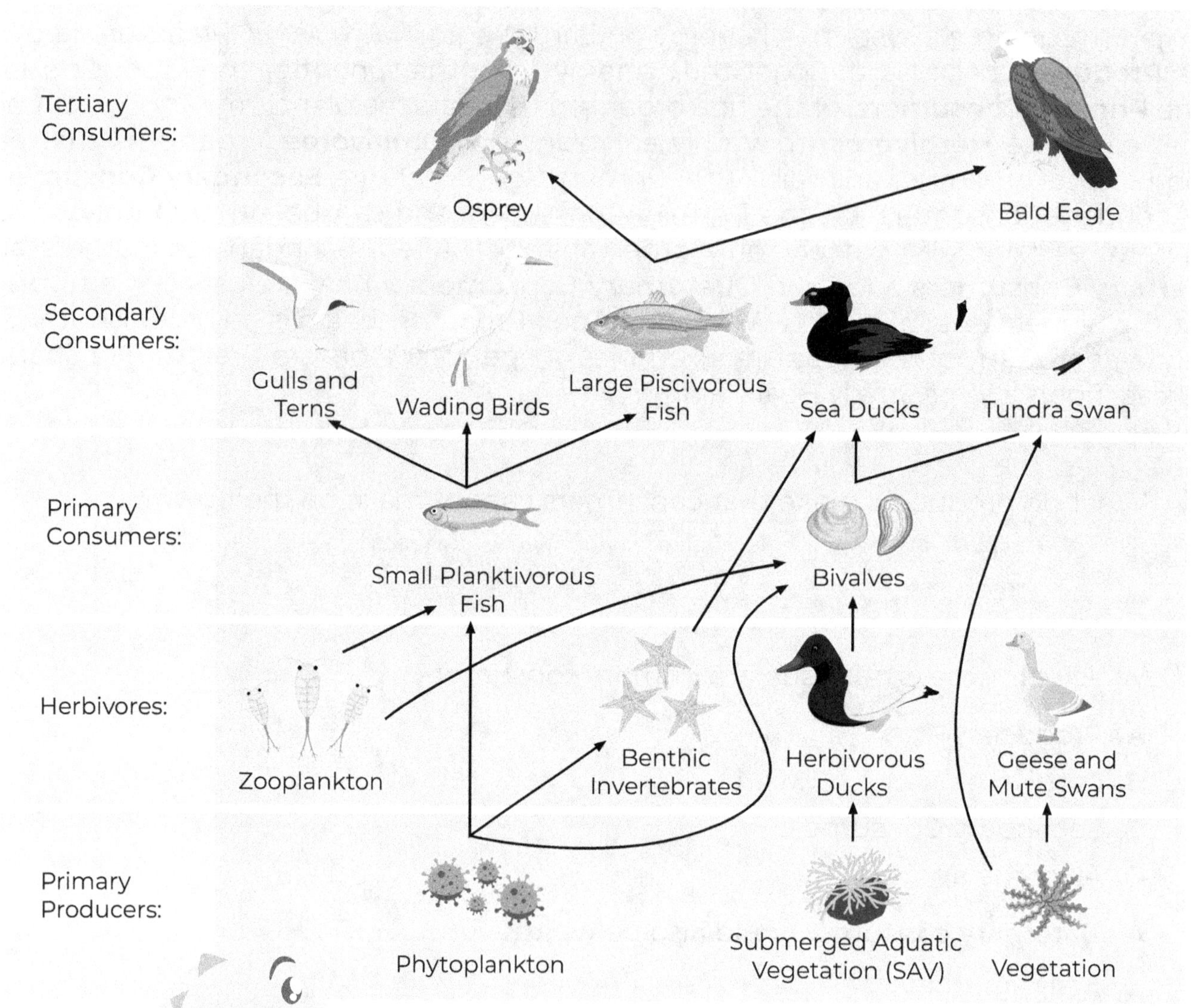

Tertiary Consumers:

Osprey   Bald Eagle

Secondary Consumers:

Gulls and Terns   Wading Birds   Large Piscivorous Fish   Sea Ducks   Tundra Swan

Primary Consumers:

Small Planktivorous Fish   Bivalves

Herbivores:

Zooplankton   Benthic Invertebrates   Herbivorous Ducks   Geese and Mute Swans

Primary Producers:

Phytoplankton   Submerged Aquatic Vegetation (SAV)   Vegetation

1. Trace the Bald Eagle's food all the way back. What food source is at the beginning of the food web for the Bald Eagle?

2. The Herbivorous Ducks are both a Primary Consumer and what else?

    A. Tertiary Consumer

    B. Quaternary Consumer

    C. Producer

    D. Herbivore

3. The Bald Eagle is also known as a(n)

    A. Herbivore

    B. Apex Predator

    C. Vegetarian

    D. Omnivore

4. A predator of Small Planktivorous Fish is:

    A. Zooplankton

    B. Benthic Invertebrates

    C. Gulls and Terns

    D. Osprey

Yesterday you analyzed a food web from the Chesapeake Bay. Today you will practice making your own food web based on your research.

Directions: Choose an Ecosystem (example: The Costa Rican Rainforest) and research the plants and animals that live there. Then make a Food Web using plants and animals that you would find there. Use arrows to show which organisms eat which other organisms, similar to the food web you examined yesterday. Put your research in the appropriate spaces below.

1. Choose an Ecosystem:

2. Research three plants that live in that Ecosystem. These are the Producers in your Food Web.

   A.

   B.

   C.

3. Research three Herbivores that live in that Ecosystem. These will be the Primary Consumers in your Food Web. Try to find ones that eat the plants you listed above.

   A.

   B.

   C.

4. Research three Omnivores that live in that Ecosystem. These will be the Secondary Consumers in your Food Web. Try to find animals that eat the plants and animals you listed in questions 2 and 3.

   A.

   B.

   C.

5. Research two to four Carnivores that live in that Ecosystem. These will be the Tertiary and Quaternary Consumers in your Food Web. Try to find animals that eat the other animals you listed in questions 3 and 4.

   A.

   B.

   C.

   D.

6. Draw your Food Web. Label all of your Trophic Levels (Producer, Primary Consumer, Secondary Consumer, Tertiary Consumer, Quaternary Consumer), make sure all arrows point in the right direction and label any Apex Predators.

Yesterday you created a food web based on research you completed on an ecosystem of your choosing. Today you will go out into nature and find the living food webs that surround you every day!

Directions: If you aren't able to go outside, that's okay. You can find images of the plants and animals that live in your local ecosystem online to do this project virtually. No matter where you live, whether your local environment is urban, suburban, rural, mountainous, coastal, forested, or a city scape, there are plants and animals all around you fighting for survival. For this project you will need the following:

Materials:

1. Camera (or phone with a camera)
2. Notebook
3. Pencil
4. This workbook

Procedure:

1. In your local ecosystem, go for a walk and see how many different plants and animals you can find. (Remember to walk safely with others and be aware of your surroundings!)

2. Take a picture of each one you see. (Remember, you can also find images online from your home ecosystem.)

    * It is best when looking for animals to be as quiet as possible so you don't scare them away.

3. Answer the following questions:

    · How many Producers did you find? ....
    · How many Herbivores did you find? ....
    · How many Omnivores did you find? ....
    · How many Carnivores did you find? ....

4. Once you have a good collection of plants and animals, make a Food Web collage of the images you found. Draw arrows in the direction of energy flow from what is being eaten to who is eating it (i.e. arrow from dandelion pointing to rabbit).

5. Label each one with their Trophic Levels.

Follow-Up Questions:

1. During your nature walk, which Trophic Level did you see the least amount of? Why do you think this is?

....

....

2. Can a food web exist without producers?

   A. Yes

   B. No

3. What type of consumer are you? What type of diet do you have?

....

....

WEEK 9

Life Science
Resource Availability in Ecosystems

MS-LS2-1

Analyze and interpret data to provide evidence for the effects of resource availability on organisms and populations of organisms in an ecosystem.

ARGOPREP

Directions: Read the text below. Then answer the questions that follow.

Disrupting Food Webs

You already know that Food Webs help us see how different types of organisms interact with each other in an ecosystem, but what happens when part of that Food Web is taken away? Sometimes, a certain species has its numbers reduced because of illness, human interaction, or natural disaster. This can lead to a plant or animal becoming **endangered** or even **extinct**. When extinction occurs, it can affect everything else in the Food Web since all of the plants and animals are interconnected. There are many examples of this happening in the world right now, and sometimes it is because of an **invasive species**. An invasive species is a plant or animal that lives in a different part of the world but was introduced to a new ecosystem where it doesn't belong because of human interference or a natural disaster.

Once it is in the new, foreign ecosystem, the invasive species disrupts the natural Food Web and can outcompete native plants and animals for food and space. Since the invasive species has no predators in its new home, it will grow out of control and continue to destroy the native ecosystem. If the organism that is affected is an **apex predator**, then something called a **Trophic Cascade** can occur. A Trophic Cascade is when the dynamic of a food web is altered due to the missing predator. Different tropic levels will increase and decrease, eventually leading to the demise of the ecosystem. Let's look at a real-world example of a Trophic Cascade below:

Pacific Ocean Trophic Cascade

Orcas are being hunted and echolocation is being affected by Navy SONAR.

Orcas can no longer hunt or feed young, so they begin beaching themselves due to SONAR.

Orcas numbers decline. (Orcas are Apex Predators.)

Orcas eat Sea Lions. Without Orcas, Sea Lion population increases.

Sea Lions eat Sea Otters. With the increase in Sea Lions, the Sea Otter population decreases.

Sea Otters eat Sea Urchins. Since there are fewer Sea Otters, the Sea Urchin numbers increase.

Sea Urchins eat Kelp. With an increase in Sea Urchins, Kelp Forests in Pacific are decimated.

Kelp forests provide habitat for fish, crustaceans, and other sea life.

Without Kelp forests many animals lose home and breeding grounds.

Trophic Cascade

Orcas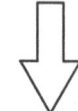

Sea Lions

Sea Otters

Sea Urchins

Kelp

1. What are three ways an organism can become endangered or extinct?

   A.

   B.

   C.

2. How does an Invasive Species affect native populations?

   A. They are stronger than native plants and animals.

   B. They outcompete native plants and animals for space and food.

   C. They bring diseases.

   D. They are more loved by people.

3. Explain how a Trophic Cascade can affect a Food Web in an Ecosystem.

Yesterday you learned about how extinction and invasive species can dramatically impact the populations of different species of organisms in an ecosystem. Today you will look at a real-life example of how two populations of organisms can cause each other's populations to change over time.

Background: Below is a graph comparing populations of Snowshoe Hare and Lynx using data collected over a period of 70 years. The lynx is an apex predator which feeds primarily on snowshoe hares. Snowshoe hares are herbivores that rely heavily on scarce vegetation in order to sustain their population. Take a moment to observe the graph and look at the peaks and valleys of the two populations.

Directions: Examine the graph data, then answer the questions that follow:

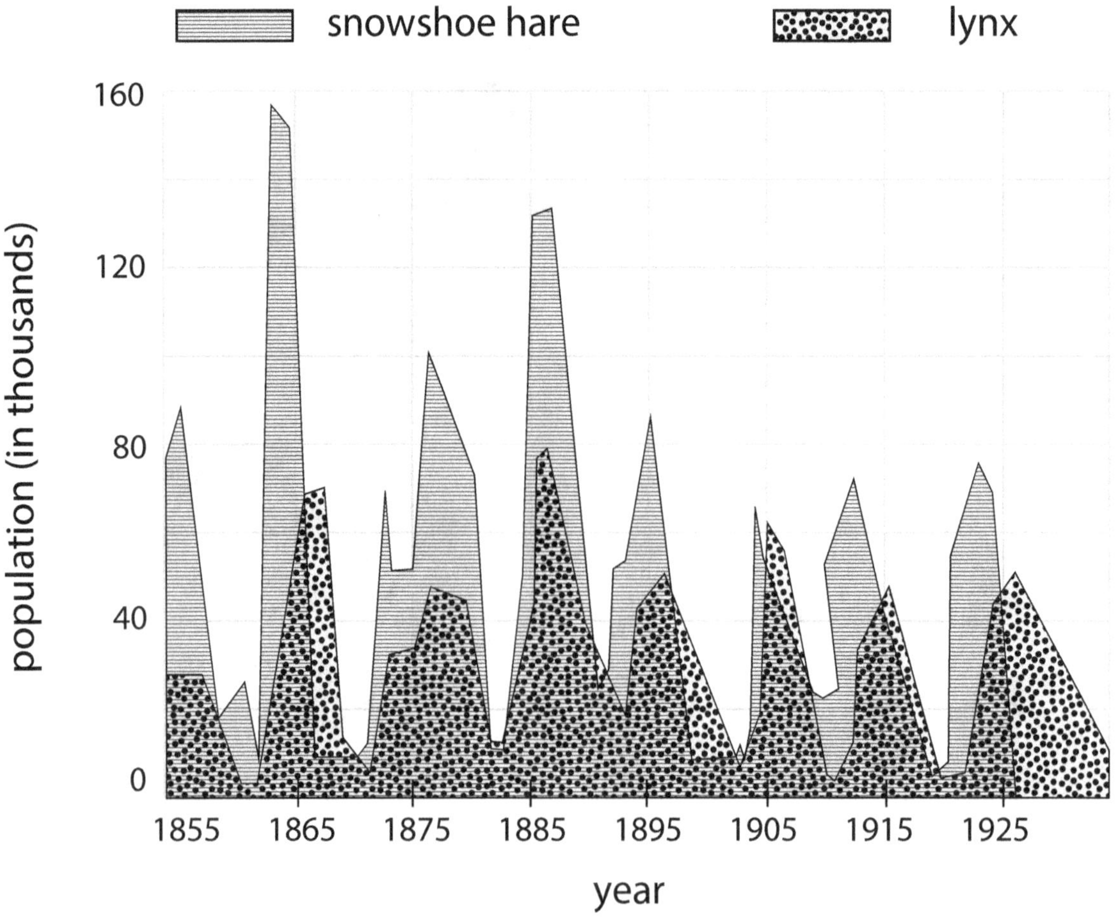

snowshoe hare   lynx

population (in thousands)

160

120

80

40

0

1855   1865   1875   1885   1895   1905   1915   1925

year

1. In what year was the population of the lynx highest?

2. During what year or years was the population of the lynx roughly 60,000 individuals or higher?

3. What is true about the relationship between the lynx population and the snowshoe hare population?

    A. When the hare population increases, the lynx population will immediately decrease.

    B. When the lynx population increases, the hare population will slowly increase.

    C. When the lynx population increases, the hare population stays the same.

    D. When the lynx population increases, the hare population slowly decreases.

4. Do these two populations have an effect on each other?

    A. Yes

    B. No

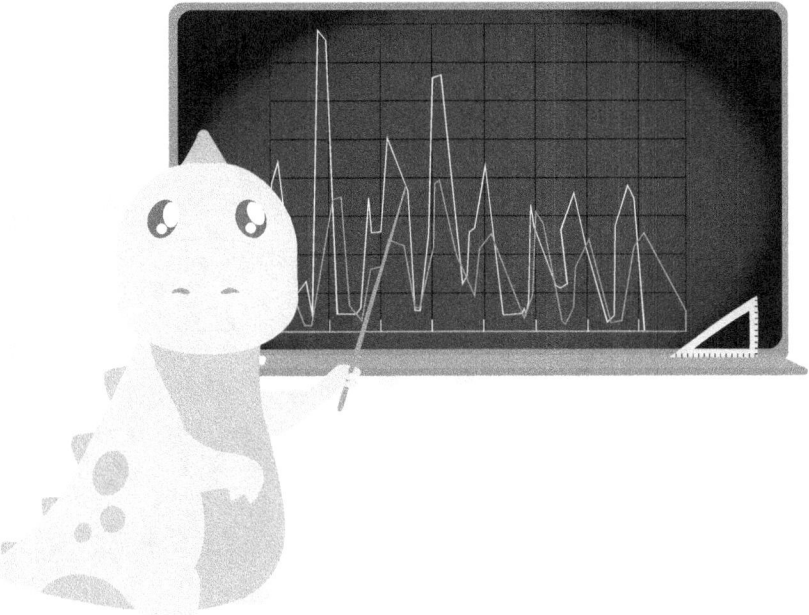

Yesterday you analyzed a graph that showed the relationship between an apex predator and its prey. Today you will explain how this graph relates to population and other aspects of this ecosystem.

Directions: Answer the questions that follow.

1. Does the lynx population ever become the same as the hare population? If so, in which year?

2. If the apex predator was removed from this ecosystem, what would happen to the population of the hare?

3. If an invasive carnivorous bobcat species was introduced to this ecosystem, how could that affect the lynx? More than one answer may be correct.

   A. The lynx population would have more competition for prey.

   B. The hare population could be completely wiped out and become endangered in this area.

   C. The lynx population could decrease.

   D. All of the above.

4. Can a change in one of these populations cause a trophic cascade?

   A. Yes

   B. No

Yesterday you explained how two populations can affect each other. Today you will complete a lab to measure the population of cardinals in an area of forest.

Directions: You will be representing a population using materials in your home. You can use any material you have on hand to represent the cardinals: pennies, Bingo chips, paper squares, or any other material. Whichever material you choose, you will need a large number of them. Any amount between 50-100 individuals is best. You will also need to mark out a quadrant on a table that is 30 cm x 30 cm (or about 12" x 12"). This is best done with masking tape.

Materials:

1. 50-100 cardinals (pennies, Bingo Chips, tiny paper squares, or some other small material)
2. Masking tape
3. A ruler measuring centimeters
4. Sharpie

Procedure:

1. Count the total number of cardinals you have in your population and write it here:
   ....

2. Randomly remove about half of the cardinals and "tag" them by putting a Sharpie X on one side. Count how many of the cardinals are tagged and write it here:
   ....

3. Measure a 30 cm by 30 cm square with your ruler and mark it on a table in masking tape. The area of your quadrant is .... sq cm.

4. Randomly place all of your cardinals on the table inside your quadrant.

5. Randomly grab a very small sample of cardinals and count how many total cardinals you captured and how many of those are tagged.

6. Record both numbers on the data table on page 94.

7. Continue for a total of "8 years" of sample trials and fill out your data table for each trial.

8. Calculate:

9. Estimated Total Population = $\dfrac{\text{(Total Number Tagged x Total Number Captured)}}{\text{Number Tagged Recaptured}}$

10. Write the Average Total Population in the last column. Calculate this by adding all of the Estimated Total Population together, and divide this sum by 8.

Cardinal Population Data Table

Year	Total # Captured	# Tagged Recaptured (marked)	Estimated Total Population
1			
2			
3			
4			
5			
6			
7			
8			
		Average Total Population:	

11. **Graph** the Estimated Total Population for 8 years (years vs. total population)

Years: 1   2   3   4   5   6   7   8   9

Yesterday you completed an experiment which showed how populations can be counted. Today you will elaborate on your data and draw conclusions.

Directions: Answer each question based on the work you have done this week on populations.

1. Write a brief summary explaining why a tagging study like the one you used in your lab is a useful tool for ornithologists. When is this technique most useful for estimating a population's size?

2. What would the Population Density of Cardinals be if the unit area were 900 square meters instead of square centimeters? Use your Average Total Population for # of individuals. Is this a realistic number for nature?

3. Imagine these are real cardinals you have been studying for almost a decade. How can seasonal changes, predator-prey relationships, invasive species, human interference, or extreme weather events help to explain any fluctuations in your 8 year study of the population? Write a short story to explain the lives of your cardinals shown on your data graph.

4. Using your graph, estimate the cardinal population for Year 9.

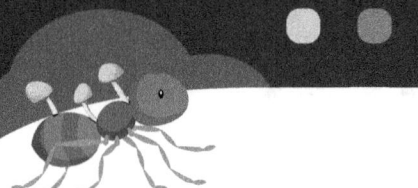

WEEK 10

Life Science

Interactions Between Organisms

MS-LS2-2

Construct an explanation that predicts patterns of interactions among organisms across multiple ecosystems.

ARGOPREP

Directions: Read the text below. Then answer the questions that follow.

How Do Organisms Interact With Each Other?

There are five main ways that organisms interact with each other in an Ecosystem: Competition, Predation, Commensalism, Mutualism, and Parasitism. All of these are types of symbiosis which just means the ways in which different species of organisms are related in a given ecosystem. With **Competition**, there aren't enough resources to go around, whether it be food, space, water, or mates. So organisms need to outcompete the others to survive, and only the strongest will live to pass their genes onto the next generation; this is survival of the fittest.

Predation is the most simplistic of the relationships, with one animal hunting and eating another animal or plant. **Commensalism** is a type of symbiosis where one organism benefits and the other is not harmed. An example of Commensalism is a cobia fish that swims underneath a Great White Shark. The shark is not harmed or helped by the cobia's presence, and it does not try to harm the cobia, but the cobia benefits from scraps of food that the shark leaves behind when it eats. The cobia also gains protection by swimming alongside such a formidable body guard. In the case of **Mutualism**, both organisms benefit from the relationship. This is the case with bees and flowers, where the flowers become pollinated, and the bees gain extra pollen and nectar to take home to feed each other and their young. The last example is **Parasitism** where one organism benefits and the other is harmed. An example of parasitism is when a mosquito bites your skin to suck your blood. You are harmed with an itchy bite while the mosquito gets a snack.

1. What are the relationships between organisms in an ecosystem called?

2. When one organism benefits and the other is neither benefited nor harmed, the relationship is called:

   A. Mutualism
   B. Parasitism
   C. Predation
   D. Commensalism

3. When both organisms benefit in a relationship, it is called:

   A. Mutualism
   B. Parasitism
   C. Predation
   D. Commensalism

Yesterday you learned about the different types of symbiotic relationships that can exist in an ecosystem. Today you will explore them further by identifying them.

Directions: Look at each of the images below, and label whether it is an example of Competition, Predation, Commensalism, Mutualism, or Parasitism. The names of the species are listed below the images. We encourage you to do some research on the Internet to learn more about each relationship if you cannot immediately identify it in the picture.

Which is Which?

A fox and a mouse

1. ....

A clown fish and
a sea anemone

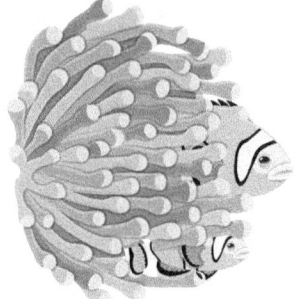

2. ....

A bison and an oxpecker

3. ....

Gazelles

4. ....

Ant and Fungus

5. ....

Yesterday you identified relationships found in different ecosystems and what type of symbiosis they represent. Today you will explain why they represent these forms of symbiosis.

Directions: Read each text below. Then answer the questions that follow.

1. The oxpecker and the bison's relationship is an example of mutualism. Why is this?

2. The two gazelles are exhibiting competition when they fight with each other. Why would two male gazelles be fighting?

3. In the relationship between the fox and the field mouse, which organism benefits?

4. What resource does the anemone provide for the clownfish?

   A. A mate
   B. Shelter
   C. Water
   D. A friend

Yesterday you continued to think about what types of symbiosis exist in nature. Today you will experiment with identifying different types of symbiotic relationships in your ecosystem!

Materials:

1. Notepad
2. Pencil
3. The internet
4. Binoculars (optional)
5. Camera or a phone that can take pictures (optional)

Directions: Today, go for a walk with a parent or guardian in an area where you live that has habitat for animals. This could be a park, a hiking trail, or a nature preserve. As you take your nature walk, stop to look at any interactions you notice between animals. If you can, snap a picture! When you arrive back home, identify what types of symbiosis each interaction represented. If you aren't sure, you can always do some research on the Internet.

Animals Involved	Type of Symbiosis?	Why?
Ex. A frog and a fly	Ex. Predation	Ex. The frog ate the fly so only the frog benefited. (The fly died.)

Yesterday you observed different types of symbiosis in the ecosystem where you live. Today you will elaborate on your observations and draw some conclusions about symbiosis.

Directions: Read the following questions and answer them below.

1. Which type of symbiosis did you find the most examples of?

....

....

2. Which type of symbiosis did you find the fewest examples of?

....

....

3. Which types of symbiosis might it be hard to find examples of and why?

....

....

4. Which type of symbiosis do you practice with other organisms in your ecosystem most often?

....

....

WEEK 11

Earth & Space Science

Geologic Time Scale

MS-ESS1-4

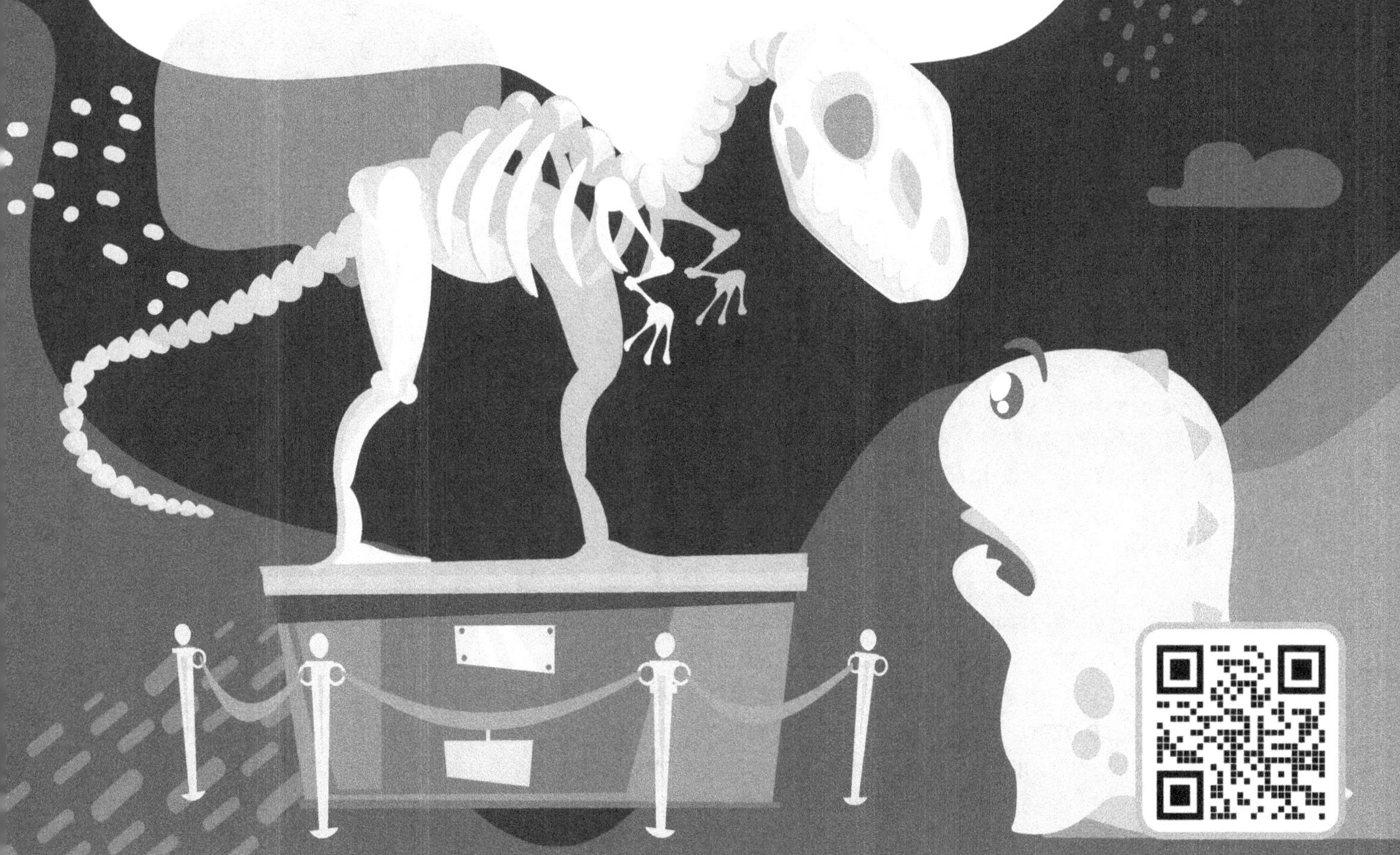

Construct a scientific explanation based on evidence from rock strata for how the geologic time scale is used to organize Earth's 4.6 billion-year-old history.

ARGOPREP

Directions: Read the text below. Then answer the questions that follow.

Dating the Earth

4.6 billion years ago Earth came into existence. It's hard to imagine how long ago that was! Because that is such a long span of time, scientists use the **Geologic Time Scale** to talk about major events in Earth's history. This scale is broken up into four major parts known as **Eras**.

The oldest and longest time period is the **Precambrian Era** which began with the formation of Earth 4.6 billion years ago and ended with the formation of complex multicellular organisms and a massive ice age 542 million years ago. This length of Geologic Time accounts for 90% of the Earth's history!

After the Precambrian Era came the **Paleozoic Era** when life in the oceans crawled out of the water as the first land-dwelling animals to evolve, and plants spread across the world. The Paleozoic Era lasted from 541 million years ago to 245 million years ago. This era ended with the largest mass extinction event in all of geologic history, the Permian/Triassic Extinction, where 96% of all species in the ocean and 70% of land species were wiped out. This extinction was due to massive and prolonged volcanic eruptions across Siberia which spewed out toxic gases across the Earth's atmosphere and made it impossible to breathe or find food. The eruptions also led to an increase in carbon dioxide gases in the atmosphere, creating a greenhouse effect and causing the acidification of the ocean. The animals that survived adapted to this new world by exploiting new habitats and new food sources.

244 million years ago, the **Mesozoic Era** began. This era marked the spread of life on land and the reign of dinosaurs. It also marked the most famous mass extinction 65.5 million years ago when a massive meteorite smashed into the Earth and wiped out 70% of all plant and animal species. The meteorite struck near present-day Mexico's Yucatan Peninsula, killing nearly all dinosaurs within weeks. This extinction event was so rapid and profound that it led to a clearly defined line of fossils in our Geologic Time Scale known as the K-T Boundary. Above this point, we no longer see any dinosaur fossils. The K-T Boundary, discovered in 1980, is an important tool that we can use to determine the relative age of other fossils.

The fourth era, the one we are currently living in, is known as the **Cenozoic Era.** This era began after the last extinction event 65 million years ago and continues today. The Cenozoic Era is when mammals began their evolutionary progression and humans finally made their appearance on the Earth. Many scientists believe that we are currently in the midst of another mass extinction event caused by humans due to habitat destruction, pollution, overharvesting of natural resources, spread of invasive species, climate change, increased population growth, and misuse of the Earth.

1. How old is the Earth?

   A. 4.6 million years old   **C.** 244 billion years old

   B. 65.5 million years old   **D.** 4.6 billion years old

2. The age of the Earth is measured using

   A. A Calendar   **C.** Dinosaurs

   B. A Geologic Time Scale   **D.** Volcanic Eruptions

3. Which of the four eras marked the largest mass extinction?

Yesterday you learned about the Geologic Time Scale and what makes each Era of Earth's history unique. Today you will take the geologic time scale and consider what it would look like if all of Earth's history took place in a single year!

Picturing 4.6 Billion Years

Activity: The history of the Earth is so vast that it's hard for us to even imagine it. In this activity, you will shrink the Earth's age down to a more understandable size: one year. Let's use 1980, since this is when the K-T boundary was discovered, an event you learned about in yesterday's reading.

Materials:

1. 9 different colors of crayons or colored pencils
2. The attached calendar

Procedure:

1. Make a Key by coloring in the box next to each era with a different color:

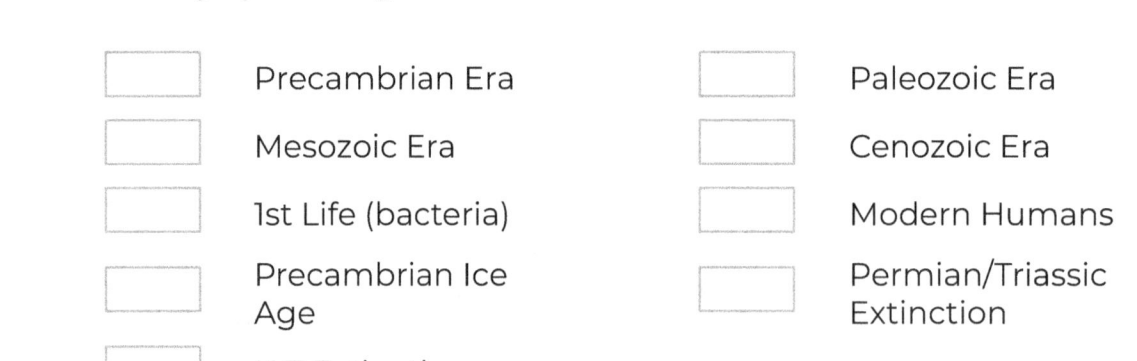

☐ Precambrian Era   ☐ Paleozoic Era

☐ Mesozoic Era   ☐ Cenozoic Era

☐ 1st Life (bacteria)   ☐ Modern Humans

☐ Precambrian Ice Age   ☐ Permian/Triassic Extinction

☐ K-T Extinction

2. March 5th is the same time period as when the first life appears. Color that day in the same color as your "1st Life" box on the calendar on page 109.

3. Color the Precambrian Era from January 1-November 22 (skipping March 5th).

4. Color November 23 the Precambrian Ice Age.

5. Color November 24-December 14 the Paleozoic Era - Fish!

6. Color December 15 the Permian/Triassic Extinction.

7. Color December 16-December 25 the Mesozoic Era - Dinosaurs!

8. Color December 26 the K-T Extinction.

9. Color December 27- most of December 31 the Cenozoic Era.

10. Color the last sliver remaining of December 31 as Modern Humans which would have appeared about 12 minutes before midnight on New Year's Eve!

Calendar of Earth

JANUARY

S	M	T	W	T	F	S
		1	2	3	4	
5	6	7	8	9	10	11
12	13	14	15	16	17	18
19	20	21	22	23	24	25
26	27	28	29	30	31	

FEBRUARY

S	M	T	W	T	F	S
						1
2	3	4	5	6	7	8
9	10	11	12	13	14	15
16	17	18	19	20	21	22
23	24	25	26	27	28	29

MARCH

S	M	T	W	T	F	S
1	2	3	4	5	6	7
8	9	10	11	12	13	14
15	16	17	18	19	20	21
22	23	24	25	26	27	28
29	30	31				

APRIL

S	M	T	W	T	F	S
		1	2	3	4	
5	6	7	8	9	10	11
12	13	14	15	16	17	18
19	20	21	22	23	24	25
26	27	28	29	30		

MAY

S	M	T	W	T	F	S
					1	2
3	4	5	6	7	8	9
10	11	12	13	14	15	16
17	18	19	20	21	22	23
24	25	26	27	28	29	30
31						

JUNE

S	M	T	W	T	F	S
	1	2	3	4	5	6
7	8	9	10	11	12	13
14	15	16	17	18	19	20
21	22	23	24	25	26	27
28	29	30				

JULY

S	M	T	W	T	F	S
		1	2	3	4	
5	6	7	8	9	10	11
12	13	14	15	16	17	18
19	20	21	22	23	24	25
26	27	28	29	30	31	

AUGUST

S	M	T	W	T	F	S
						1
2	3	4	5	6	7	8
9	10	11	12	13	14	15
16	17	18	19	20	21	22
23	24	25	26	27	28	29
30	31					

SEPTEMBER

S	M	T	W	T	F	S
		1	2	3	4	5
6	7	8	9	10	11	12
13	14	15	16	17	18	19
20	21	22	23	24	25	26
27	28	29	30			

OCTOBER

S	M	T	W	T	F	S
				1	2	3
4	5	6	7	8	9	10
11	12	13	14	15	16	17
18	19	20	21	22	23	24
25	26	27	28	29	30	31

NOVEMBER

S	M	T	W	T	F	S
1	2	3	4	5	6	7
8	9	10	11	12	13	14
15	16	17	18	19	20	21
22	23	24	25	26	27	28
29	30					

DECEMBER

S	M	T	W	T	F	S
		1	2	3	4	5
6	7	8	9	10	11	12
13	14	15	16	17	18	19
20	21	22	23	24	25	26
27	28	29	30	31		

Now you have created a representation of what all of Earth's history would look like packed into one year. How incredible is that?

Yesterday you created a diagram to represent all of Earth's history in one year. Today you will look back at that model and explain what this shows you about Earth's major eras.

Directions: Read the questions and answer them below.

1. About how many months pass before we see any form of life?

2. Compared to the other eras, is the Mesozoic Era a relatively long or short period of time?

   A. Long

   B. Short

3. On which of these calendar dates would you be able to find a dinosaur?

   A. December 15th
   C. December 26th

   B. December 29th
   D. December 19th

4. Which is the longest Era?

5. In what month is the Precambrian Ice Age?

Yesterday you explained what your geologic time scale model showed you about time on Earth. Today, you will become an archaeologist at home by discovering the **strata***, the different layers of Earth, where you live!*

Dig a Strata Experiment

Directions: With an adult's permission, find a wooded area of your yard or a park to dig a small hole deep enough to see multiple layers of dirt and Earth. All you need is a garden shovel and a sense of adventure. If you live in an area where digging is not possible, visit a canyon or an area where you can see lots of exposed rock and all the different layers in it. You could also look up places like Palo Duro Canyon on the internet and observe the different stratas found in the canyon walls there. These layers were deposited over hundreds of millions of years!

1. Draw a picture of what the strata, or layers, of the soil looked like when you dug the hole. Use colors to show different layers:

2. During what era of Earth's history do you think these layers of soil and rock formed? Why do you think that?

....

....

....

3. Why is it unlikely that you dug a hole in soil or rocks that were created during the Precambrian era?

....

....

....

4. When we go deeper into the Earth's crust, is the dirt older?

A. Yes

B. No

Newest layer

Oldest layer

Yesterday you learned about the Law of Superposition by exploring different layers of rock and dirt. Today you will elaborate on your experience and findings.

Directions: Read and think about each of the questions below, and answer in complete sentences.

1. What do you think these layers tell you about what might have been here before? For example, where there is a layer of sand, the land may have once been an ocean. If there is clay, it may have once been covered in a swamp.

2. Did you find anything unexpected when you were digging? Welcome to the exciting work of an archaeologist! Write about your experience here.

3. Imagine it is the year 5120. The ways of our civilization are long gone, and most of our history is forgotten. If you were an archaeologist uncovering the past in what is currently your hometown, describe what sorts of things you would find over a thousand years later that might help you piece together what life might have been like for the people living there.

Earth & Space Science

Rock Layers

MS-ESS2-1

Develop a model to describe the cycling of Earth's materials and the flow of energy that drives this process.

Directions: Read the text below. Then answer the questions that follow.

The Earth Rocks!

When making a cake, you know that the layer on the bottom has to be put on the plate before frosting it, and then the next layer can be put on top, followed by more frosting. You can't decorate the cake before you put it together. Just like a delicious layer cake, the Earth is made up of layers of rock known as **strata**, which you learned a bit about last week. This layering happens in a specific order, with the oldest layers on the bottom and newer layers piled on top. This is known as the **Law of Superposition**. The types of layers of rock that make up the Earth are based on the specific environment that was present at the time they developed. For example, the ground of the Sahara Desert is very different from the ground of the Amazon Rainforest, and both of these are different from the ground in Hawaii. Different places under different conditions result in different kinds of layers of the Earth. The types of rocks present on Earth can be broken down into three main categories: Metamorphic Rock, Igneous Rock, and Sedimentary Rock.

Metamorphic Rocks are formed deep in the Earth's crust where there is a lot of pressure and heat. Examples of Metamorphic Rocks are: Shale, Slate, Gneiss, Marble, Anthracite, Soapstone, and Schist.

Igneous Rocks are formed near volcanoes from cooling lava or magma. There are two main categories of Igneous Rocks: Extrusive and Intrusive. Extrusive rocks form on the surface of the Earth when molten hot magma escapes from a volcano in the form of lava and cools on the surface of the earth's crust. Intrusive rocks form inside of the Earth's crust when magma cools and solidifies before it has the chance to escape. Examples of Igneous Rocks are: Basalt, Granite, Gabbro, Pumice, Obsidian, and Quartzite.

Sedimentary Rock forms when loose sediment and debris are pushed together for a very long time so they are compacted together to form rock. These rocks are the only types of rocks that can contain fossils and are typically formed through erosion and weathering from wind and water. Examples of Sedimentary Rocks are: Limestone, Chalk, Flint, and Sandstone.

1. The oldest layers of rocks are

   A. On the surface of the earth's crust   **C.** The lowest layer of rocks

   B. Right below the top layer   **D.** Unknown

2. Extrusive Igneous rocks form when

   A. There is magma that cools under the Earth's crust

   B. There is a lot of pressure and heat inside of the Earth's crust

   C. There are loose sediments and other materials that get compacted together for a long time to form rock

   D. There is lava that cools on the surface of the Earth

3. Sedimentary rocks form when

   A. There is magma that cools under the Earth's crust

   B. There is lava that cools on the surface of the Earth

   C. There are loose sediments and other materials that get compacted together for a long time to form rock

   D. There is a lot of pressure and heat inside of the Earth's crust

Yesterday you learned about the different types of rock that make up the Earth. Today you will learn about the Rock Cycle and how different kinds of rock are formed.

Directions: Analyze the diagram and read the text below. Then answer the questions that follow.

The Rock Cycle

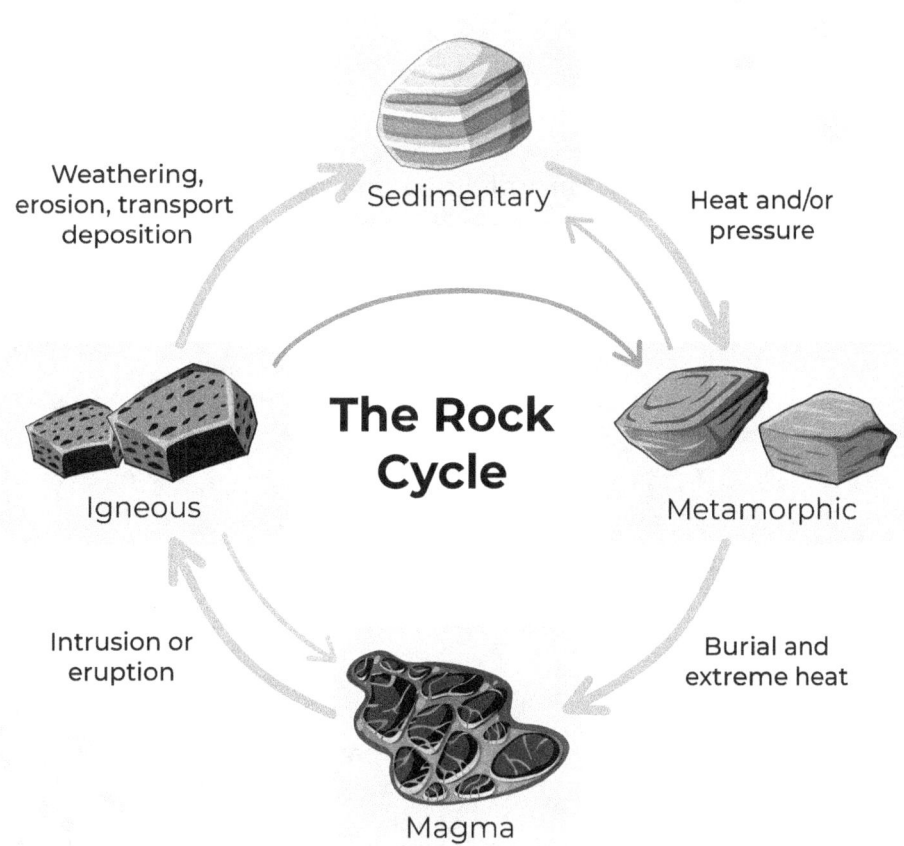

The Rock Cycle begins and ends with Magma. This is the molten rock layer below the Earth's crust where Igneous Rock is formed at volcanoes. After time and erosion, Extrusive Igneous Rock can break down into Sedimentary Rock. Following the red line, Igneous Rock that is intrusive and is underground can be exposed to heat and pressure under the earth's surface and become Metamorphic Rock. An example of an Igneous Rock turning into Metamorphic Rock is Granite into Gneiss. Sedimentary Rock can also become buried over time and turn into Metamorphic Rock. An example of a Sedimentary Rock turning into Metamorphic Rock is Limestone into Marble. A Metamorphic Rock can turn back into a Sedimentary Rock through weathering, erosion, or chemical breakdown. The cycle repeats when Metamorphic Rock is melted back into magma and is repurposed as new Igneous Rock.

1. What type of rock can limestone, a type of metamorphic rock, turn into?

2. Extrusive Igneous Rock breaks down into what kind of rock?

3. Can a metamorphic rock turn directly into an igneous rock?

Yesterday you learned about the Rock Cycle. Today you will explain in more detail how the rock cycle works.

Directions: Read the questions and answer below.

1. Why is the Rock cycle considered a cycle? Think about what the term cycle means.

2. Can Igneous Rock ever turn directly into magma? Why or why not?

3. What causes sedimentary rock to break down?

4. Is it possible to find magma at the surface of Earth? Why or why not?

Yesterday you explained how the rock cycle works and why it is a cycle. Today you will model the rock cycle using sugar, a crystal that can go through similar stages as the rocks in the Rock Cycle but in far less time!

Materials:

1. 1 Tealight Candle
2. 1 Lighter or Match
3. 1 Sugar Cube
4. 1 6" Piece of Aluminum Foil Folded into the shape of a small bowl
5. Tongs for holding the foil bowl
6. Oven mitts
7. Goggles (strongly recommended)

NOTE: Please have a parent or guardian around when working with fire and hot sugar! It can burn you, so please wear protective eyewear and gloves.

Procedure & Questions:

1. Examine the sugar cube before you begin and record your observations.

Draw Observations:	What type of rock does the sugar cube represent?
	Explain why you think this:

2. Scratch the edge of the sugar cube with your finger and record your observations.

Draw Observations:	What process in the rock cycle does scratching the sugar represent?
	....
	....
	....
	....

3. Place the sugar cube in the bowl you made out of your foil, and hold the bowl with the tongs over the candle's flame. Pass the bowl slowly back and forth. Record your observations below.

....

....

....

4. While holding the bowl directly over the candle flame with the tongs, observe as the sugar begins to melt. Record your observations.

Draw Observations:	What **process** in the rock cycle does this represent?
	....
	What would this molten rock be called? ....

5. Set the foil bowl aside on a safe surface away from the flame and wait 2-3 minutes. Record your observation.

Draw Observations:	What type of rock does this represent?
	....

6. Break or crush the hardened sugar into pieces once it's cooled and record your observations below.

Draw Observations:	What part of the rock cycle do the crushed pieces represent?
	....

Yesterday you experimented by using sugar to model the Rock Cycle. Today you will elaborate on the experiment and the observations you recorded.

Directions: Read and think about each of the questions below, and answer in complete sentences.

1. Why did you need to use fire and heat in the experiment? What part of the rock cycle did it represent?

2. Why was it important to use a solid form of sugar as opposed to a liquid form of sugar such as syrup or honey?

3. Explain how Igneous Rocks, Metamorphic Rocks, and Sedimentary Rocks are all related.

4. Which type of rock is most likely to result in a dinosaur fossil and why?

Earth & Space Science

Changing Earth

MS-ESS2-2

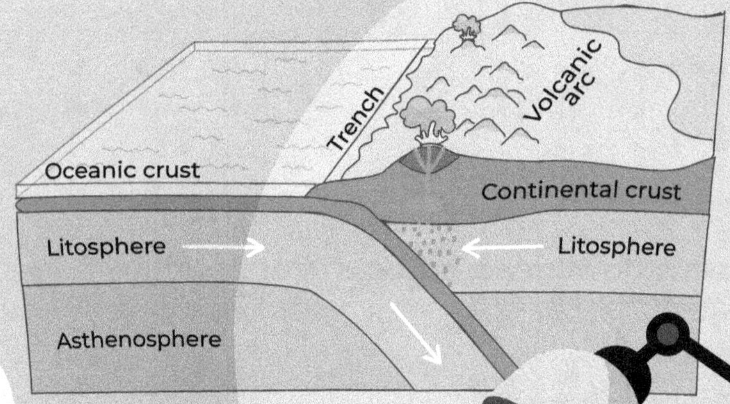

Construct an explanation based on evidence for how geoscience processes have changed Earth's surface on varying time and spatial scales.

Directions: Read the text below. Then answer the questions that follow.

Who's Fault Is It?

Earth is always changing, but what is responsible for all of these constant changes? There are some changes that we can see and feel. Volcanic eruptions on the Earth's surface are obvious indicators of changes happening both above and below the Earth. Earthquakes also help us feel when there are things going on below the Earth's surface crust. Sometimes, we can even see massive waves called **tsunamis** that are triggered by undersea earthquakes that indicate changes occurring under the ocean. But what causes each of these events? The Earth is made up of several layers: The Inner Core, Outer Core, Mantle, and Crust. The **Crust** is the part that we live on, and it is floating on top of the **mantle**, which is made of molten rock called magma. The magma is always circulating due to convection currents inside of the Earth that heat up at the Inner Core and **Outer Core** and cool down at the Crust. The Crust is not solid but is broken into 12 pieces called **Plates**. The movement of the Earth's crust, including events like volcanoes and earthquakes, is caused by areas where pieces of the crust meet each other. These are called **Fault Boundaries.**

1. True or false: Earth is always changing, even if we cannot see the changes on the Earth's surface.

   A. True   **B.** False

2. How are tsunamis made?

   A. Magma   **C.** Volcanos

   B. Large cruise ships   **D.** Underwater earthquakes

3. What do you call the areas where pieces of the Earth's crust meet?

   A. Mantle

   B. Fault Boundaries

   C. Plates

   D. Inner core

Yesterday you learned about the changes Earth goes through and how the crust that we live on is made of plates that are constantly moving around. Today you will learn more about the types of fault boundaries that exist in the Earth's crust.

Directions: Look at the diagrams below and read the adjacent text. Then answer the questions that follow.

There are 3 types of Faults: Strike-Slip Fault, Normal Fault, and Reverse Fault. Each type of fault is the result of plates on the crust sliding past each other, pushing against each other, or moving away from each other. The result can lead to earthquakes and volcanoes. Moving plates can also create islands and mountains, as well as move entire continents or destroy seafloors. A **Strike-Slip Fault** is when two plates move side to side opposite each other. Examples of Strike-Slip Faults are the San-Andreas Fault in California and the Anatolian Fault in Turkey.

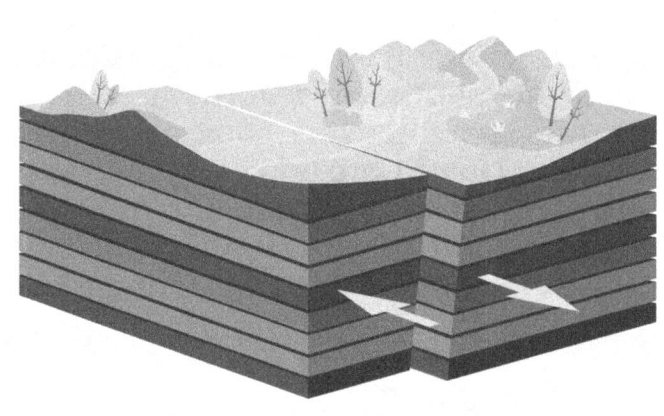

A **Normal Fault** is when two plates move away from each other and make a valley between them. The Mid Atlantic Ridge in the center of the Atlantic Ocean is the most prominent example of this. It is what led to the movement of the continents and continues to move the continents apart to this day. The East African Rift Valley separates eastern Africa from the rest of the continent, so eventually a new ocean will form there.

Reverse Faults do the opposite of a Normal Fault and push the plates together. When this happens, two possibilities can occur. If it happens on land, one of the plates slides on top of another, forming a mountain ridge or a volcano. An example of this is the Himalayan Mountains.

If it happens along a coastline, the heavier oceanic plate falls under the lighter continental plate and a type of Reverse Fault called a **Subduction Zone** forms. The older, heavier oceanic plate is reformed into magma along the falling edge. The continental plate above is subjected to the formation of mountains, volcanoes, and earthquakes. This happens along the Pacific Plate boundary, an area known as "The Ring of Fire." A mountain range which has formed along a Subduction Zone is the Rocky Mountains.

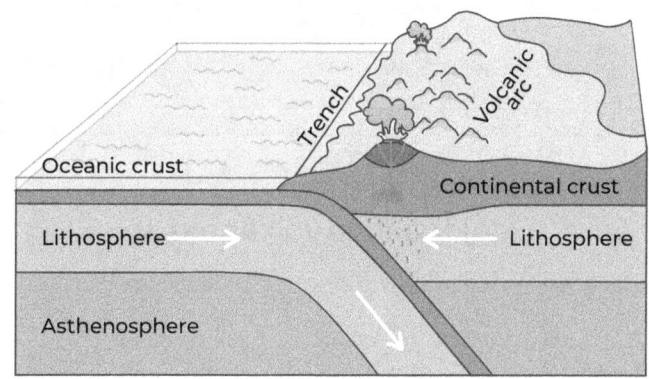

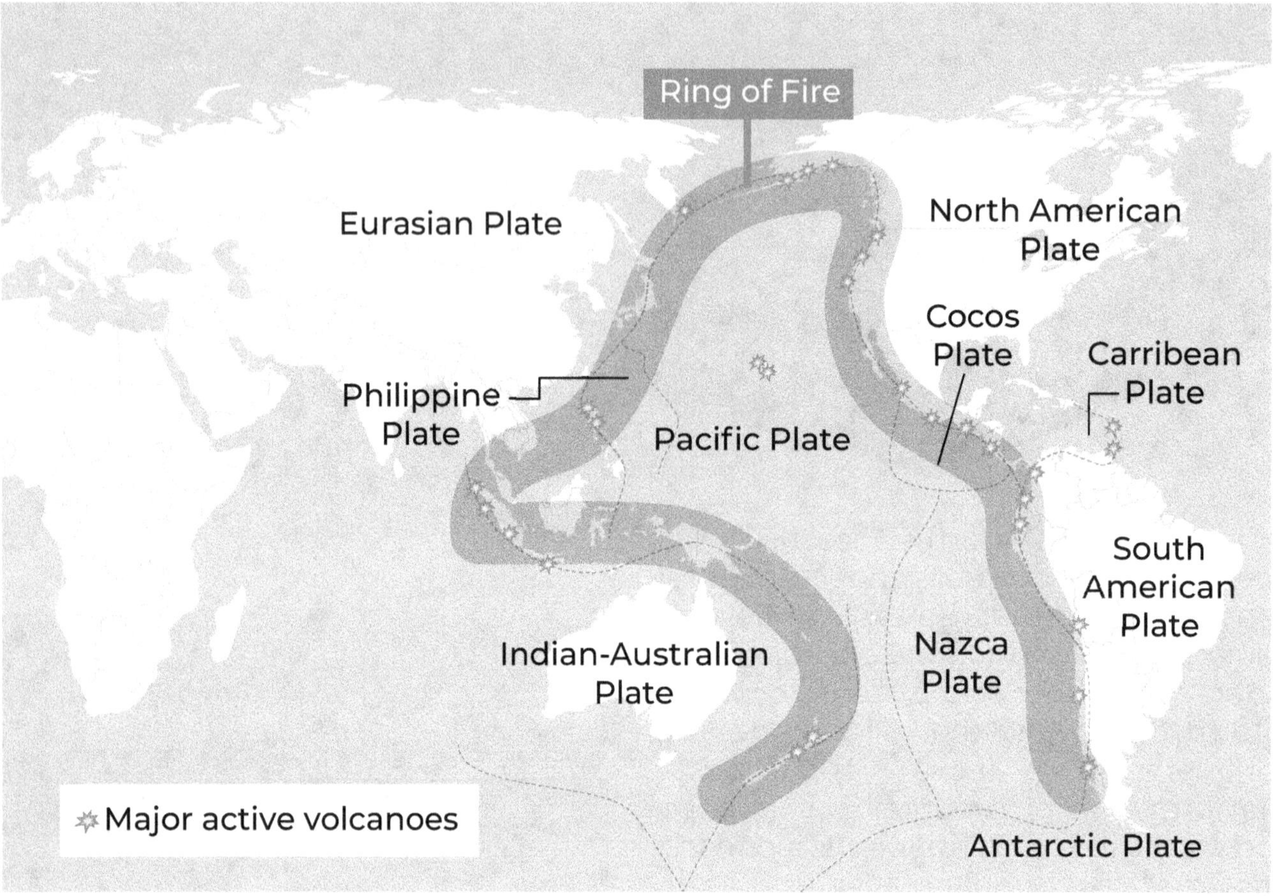

Ring of Fire

Eurasian Plate

North American Plate

Cocos Plate

Carribean Plate

Philippine Plate

Pacific Plate

South American Plate

Indian-Australian Plate

Nazca Plate

✳ Major active volcanoes

Antarctic Plate

1. What type of fault is shown in the image below?

A. Strike-Slip Fault

B. Normal Fault

C. Reverse Fault

D. Subduction Zone

2. What type of fault is shown in the image below?

A. Strike Slip Fault

B. Normal Fault

C. Reverse Fault

D. Subduction Zone

Yesterday you learned about the different types of faults the Earth's crust contains. Today you will explain how these faults work and what types of change can occur at them.

Directions: Read and answer the questions that follow.

1. If two plates were to move away from each other, what would form between them?

   A. A mountain   **C.** A volcano

   B. A valley   **D.** A subduction zone

2. Is it more dangerous or less dangerous to build a home right on top of a fault boundary as opposed to the center of a plate?

   A. More dangerous

   B. Less dangerous

3. At what type of fault boundary is magma created from an older, heavier plate?

   A. Slip-strike fault

   B. Reverse Fault

   C. Normal Fault

   D. Magma fault

4. Research the Corinth Rift in Greece. What type of fault is it?

Yesterday you explained the differences between the three fault types in the Earth's crust. Today you will experiment with fault types by demonstrating how they move using tasty treats!

Directions: Read each text below. Then answer the questions that follow.

Materials:

1. Graham Crackers (3 whole crackers)
2. Spoonful of Whipped Cream (like Cool Whip) - Frosting or Fluff works too
3. Pie Plate or Plate
4. 1 piece of bread

Procedure:

Make a Normal Fault:

A. Spread a thick layer of whipped cream on the plate.
B. Break a graham cracker in half along the perforation and place both pieces side by side on top.
C. Gently press down on both graham crackers while pushing them away from each other.

1. What happened to the whipped cream as you pushed down and away with the graham crackers?

....

....

....

2. What is an example of a place on earth where this occurs?

....

....

Make a Strike-Slip Fault:

A. Place two graham cracker halves on top of a layer of whipped cream on the plate side by side.
B. Press the graham crackers gently together. At the same time, push one away from you and pull the other toward you. Keep applying pressure while you do so.

3. What happened to the graham crackers while you slid them past each other?

....

....

....

4. Where is an example of a place on Earth where this occurs?

....

....

Make a Reverse Fault:

A. Put a fresh layer of whipped cream on the plate.

B. Place a piece of bread on the whipped cream, and put a whole graham cracker next to the bread.

C. Push the graham cracker against the bread while keeping the bread from moving backward.

5. What happened to the graham cracker when you pushed it against the bread?

....

....

6. Did the bread buckle or fold at any point?

A. Yes

B. No

Yesterday you experimented with modeling different types of faults using graham crackers, whipped cream and bread. Today you will elaborate on your observations.

Directions: Read and think about each of the questions below, and answer in complete sentences.

1. What did the whipped cream represent?

   ....

   ....

   ....

2. For the reverse fault, you used both bread and graham crackers to represent different kinds of plates. What types of plates did each of these represent?

   ....

   ....

   ....

3. Remember that when the Earth changes, it can sometimes cause movement that we can feel such as an Earthquake. How could you model this in the experiment you did yesterday?

   ....

   ....

   ....

4. Can you think of another way to model the different kinds of faults and their movement? What other materials could you use and why?

   ....

   ....

   ....

   ....

   ....

Earth & Space Science

Pangaea & Seafloor Spreading

MS-ESS2-3

Analyze and interpret data on the distribution of fossils and rocks, continental shapes, and seafloor structures to provide evidence of the past plate motions.

Directions: Read the text below. Then answer the questions that follow.

The Biggest Puzzle

Take a look at a map of the world. If you are like many people, you may notice the continents appear to fit together like a giant puzzle. This is not a new concept. For a long time, people have noticed the continents seemed to fit together, but didn't think much of it. Then, in 1915, a meteorologist named Alfred Wegener published a scientific paper on research he had been collecting supporting **Continental Drift Hypothesis**. Wegener proposed that the continents looked like they fit together because at one time they actually did! He sought to prove this by comparing fossilized animal, plant, and rock specimens from around the world. The map below from USGS shows the fossil evidence he collected.

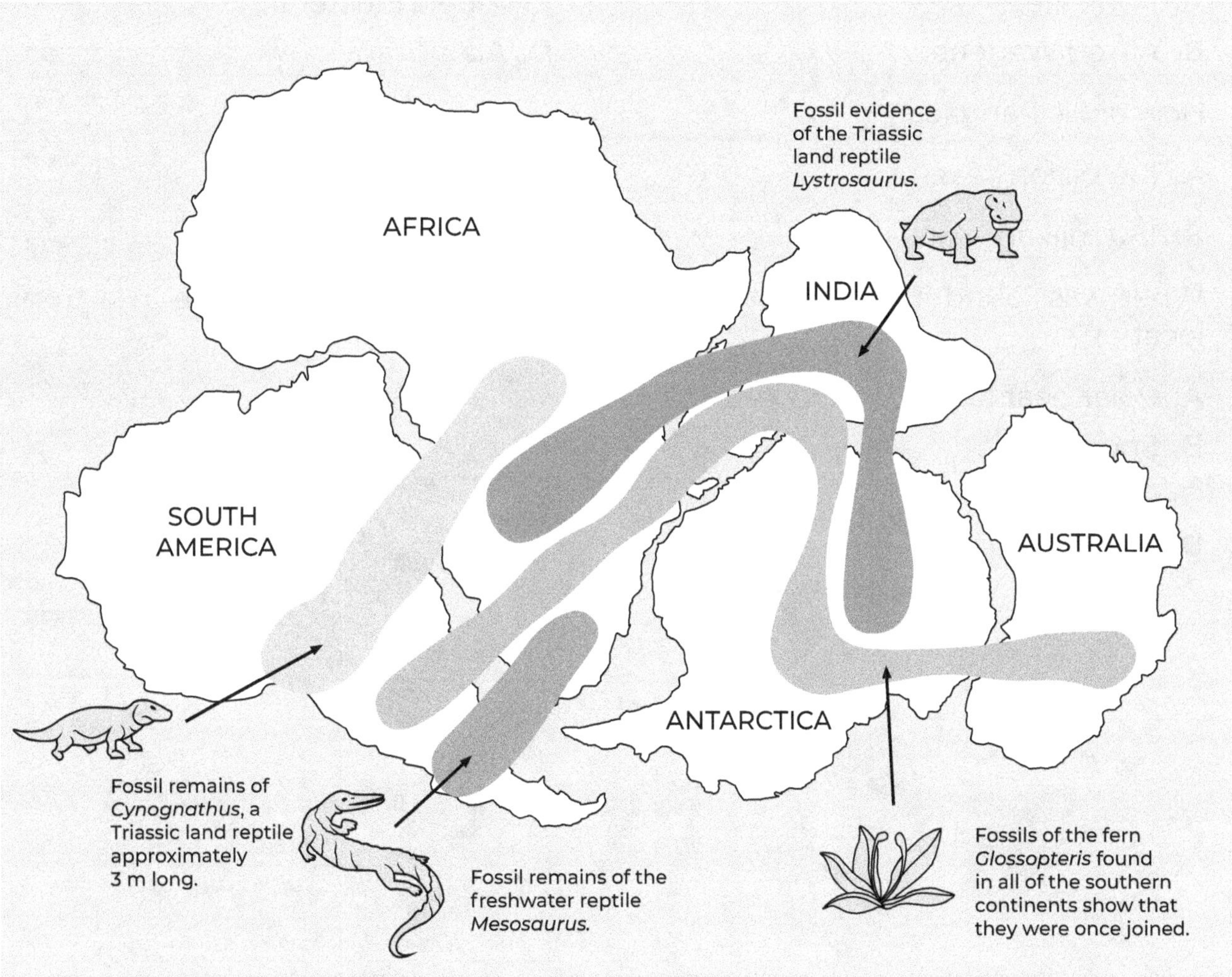

AFRICA

Fossil evidence
of the Triassic
land reptile
Lystrosaurus.

INDIA

SOUTH
AMERICA

AUSTRALIA

ANTARCTICA

Fossil remains of
Cynognathus, a
Triassic land reptile
approximately
3 m long.

Fossil remains of the
freshwater reptile
Mesosaurus.

Fossils of the fern
Glossopteris found
in all of the southern
continents show that
they were once joined.

In addition to this fossil evidence comparing plant and animal species, Wegener also found tropical plant species fossilized in frigid Norway, proving that it must have once been located in a more tropical location. He found that South America and Africa contained the same geological makeup, and the Appalachian Mountain Range of eastern North America was geologically related to the Caledonian Mountains of Scotland. Alfred Wegener called this supercontinent "**Pangaea**," and it existed 280 million years ago. It began breaking apart 180 million years ago, and it took many millions of years for the continents to move into the places we currently know them to be.

1. The name of the scientist who proposed Continental Drift Hypothesis was

   A. Harry Hess

   B. Alfred Wegener

   C. Albert Einstein

   D. Alan Grant

2. How old is Pangaea?

   A. 180 billion years

   B. 180 million years

   C. 280 million years

   D. 280 billion years

3. What was found in Norway that showed this country used to be in a tropical location?

   A. Polar bear fossils

   B. Snow

   C. Plant fossils

   D. Insects in amber

Yesterday you learned about the Continental Drift Hypothesis and the supercontinent of Pangaea. Today you will try to piece the current continents back together to see what Pangaea may have looked like before it broke apart.

Directions: Read each text below. Then answer the questions that follow.

Piecing Pangaea

Just like the geologists, philosophers, and scientists who came before you, today you will observe a map of the Earth and fit the pieces together like a puzzle. Make a copy of the map on this page, and cut out the continents as close to the edges as possible. Cut apart every continent separately, even if they look connected on the map. Try to piece them together like a puzzle; how do you think they might have fit as one big continent 200 million years ago?

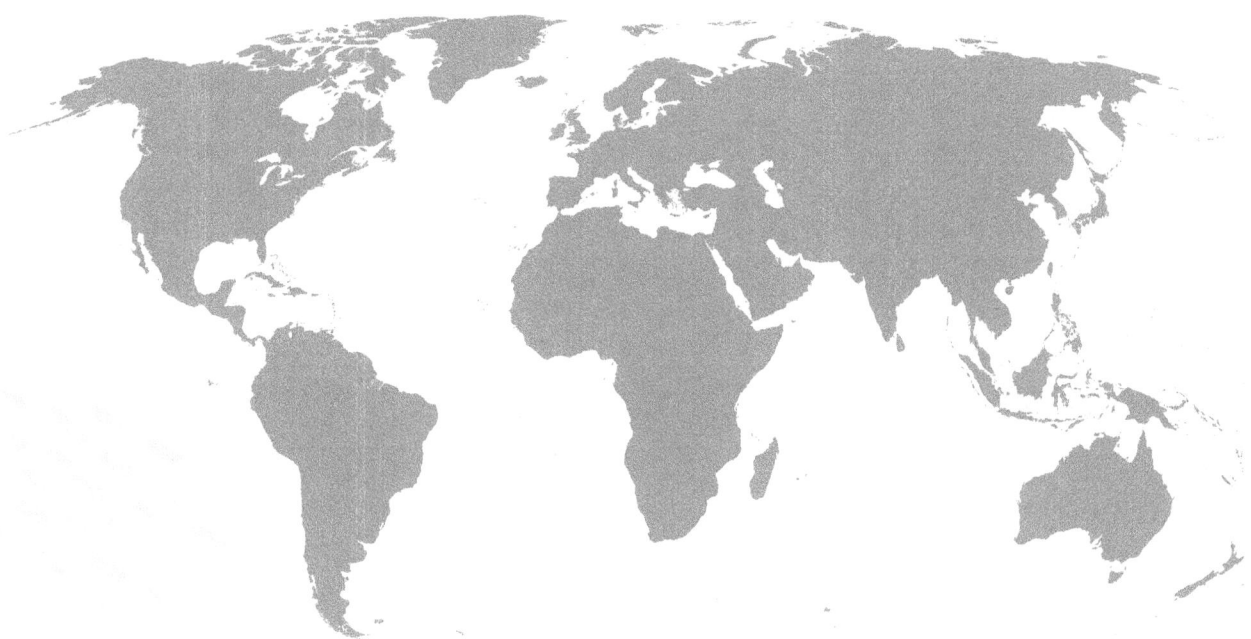

1. Which two continents fit together the best?

2. Not all of the pieces fit together exactly right, what do you think might account for the continents not fitting perfectly?

Yesterday you explored how Pangaea may have looked before it broke apart. Today you will explain that phenomenon in more detail by learning about seafloor spreading.

Directions: Read each text below. Then answer the questions that follow.

In the Trenches

Seafloor Spreading is when new crust is formed in the oceans. It was ultimately what caused the different plates of Pangaea to break apart and begin to move away from each other. Seafloor Spreading created our modern day continents and continues to cause them to slowly drift. There are two ways that these different crusts can meet: passive plate margins and active plate margins.

A **passive plate** margin is found along the Mid-Atlantic Ridge where the Oceanic Crust of the North American Plate meets the Continental Crust of Eastern North America. There is no Subduction Zone (see Week 13) here, so the spreading just pushes these continents farther apart, making the Atlantic Ocean larger in the process. This caused the supercontinent of Pangaea to break apart and resulted in Continental Drift. On the opposite side of the world is an **active plate** margin. The East Pacific Rise is responsible for creating new crust in the Pacific Ocean that spreads out very quickly and is recycled even faster, returning back to the Earth as magma to become new crust again. The area where the recycling occurs is where the Oceanic Crust meets the surrounding Continental Plates. This area is called a Subduction Zone and is shaped like a horeshoe, giving it the nickname "The Ring of Fire." Along the Subduction Zones, there are also volcanoes, earthquakes, and tsunamis.

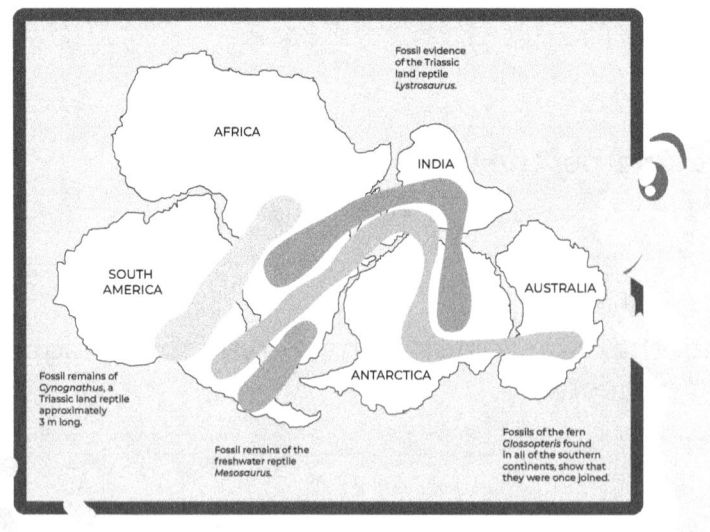

1. Take a look at the map of Pangaea you made yesterday. Identify at least two places where seafloor spreading began taking place.

2. What becomes new crust eventually and is usually "recycled" at active plate margins?

3. On your map of Pangaea from yesterday, circle where you think the passive plate margin is that eventually created the Mid-Atlantic Ridge.

4. On your map of Pangaea from yesterday, circle where you think the active plate margin is that eventually created the East Pacific Rise where "The Ring of Fire" can be found today.

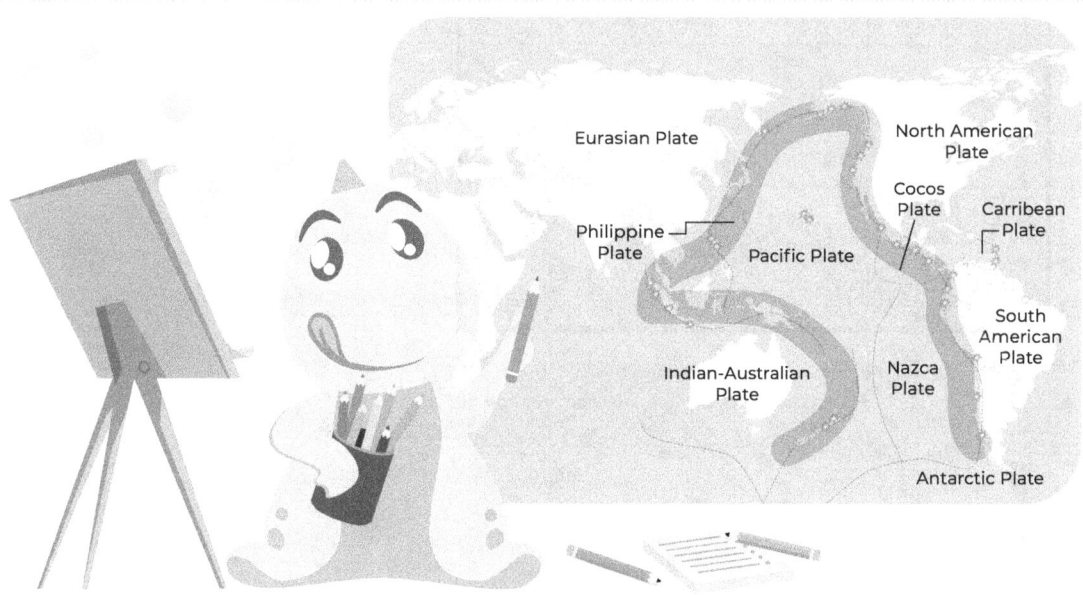

Yesterday you learned about seafloor spreading and how it caused Pangaea to break apart while continuing to facilitate continental drift. Today you will experiment with the new concept of trenches and analyze a map for information about a specific trench, the Mariana Trench.

Directions: Read each text below. Then answer the questions that follow.

What Are Trenches?

There are trenches in every ocean, but the deepest ocean trenches are located at the Subduction Zones along the Pacific Plate. The deepest part of the ocean is in the **Mariana Trench** which is in the Pacific Ocean off the coast of Guam. Its deepest point is known as Challenger Deep. Life in the trenches is not easy. It's ice cold and pitch black so there's no photosynthesis, and yet life finds a way. Most of the primary consumers here find food by eating marine snow, the tiny bits of decaying plant and animal matter, and waste that falls down from the ocean above. Some animals live along hydrothermal vents to keep warm and find nutrients while others hunt for food in the dark using **bioluminescence**, a natural light they make themselves.

Being so deep means life here is under a lot of pressure, about 12,400 tons per square meter and 1,000 times greater than the pressure on the surface. Because of this, most of the animals have very blobby bodies and wouldn't survive in shallow water, just like the animals living in the shallows couldn't survive so deep. They would be crushed!

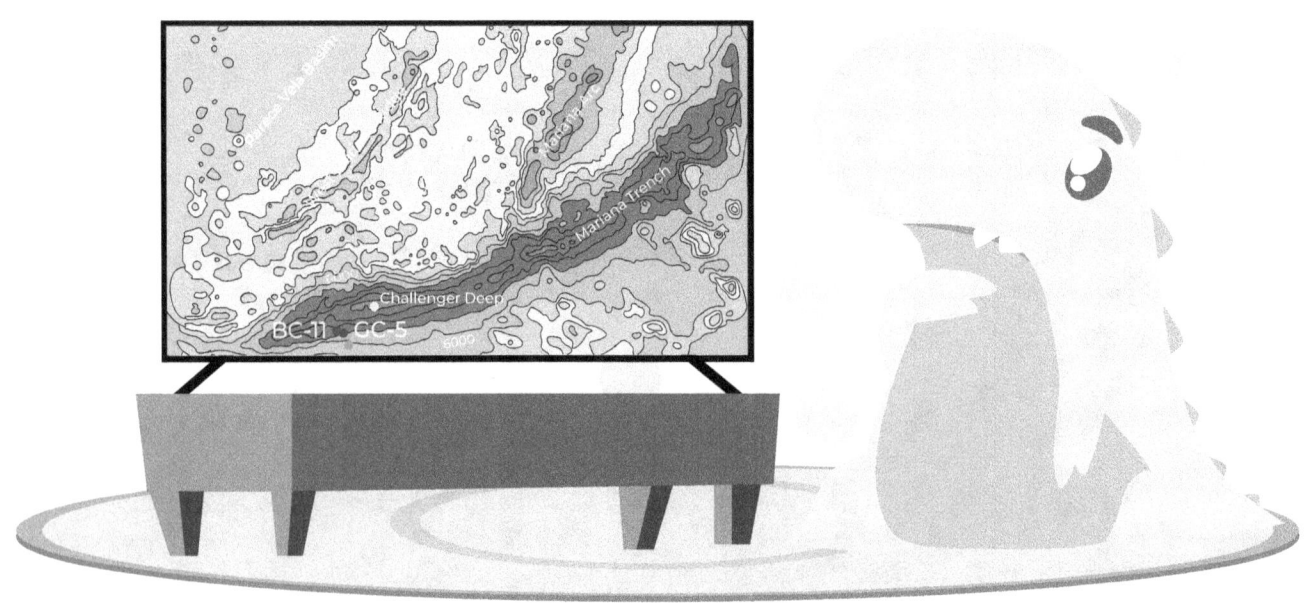

Take a look at this Bathymetric Map of the Mariana Trench:

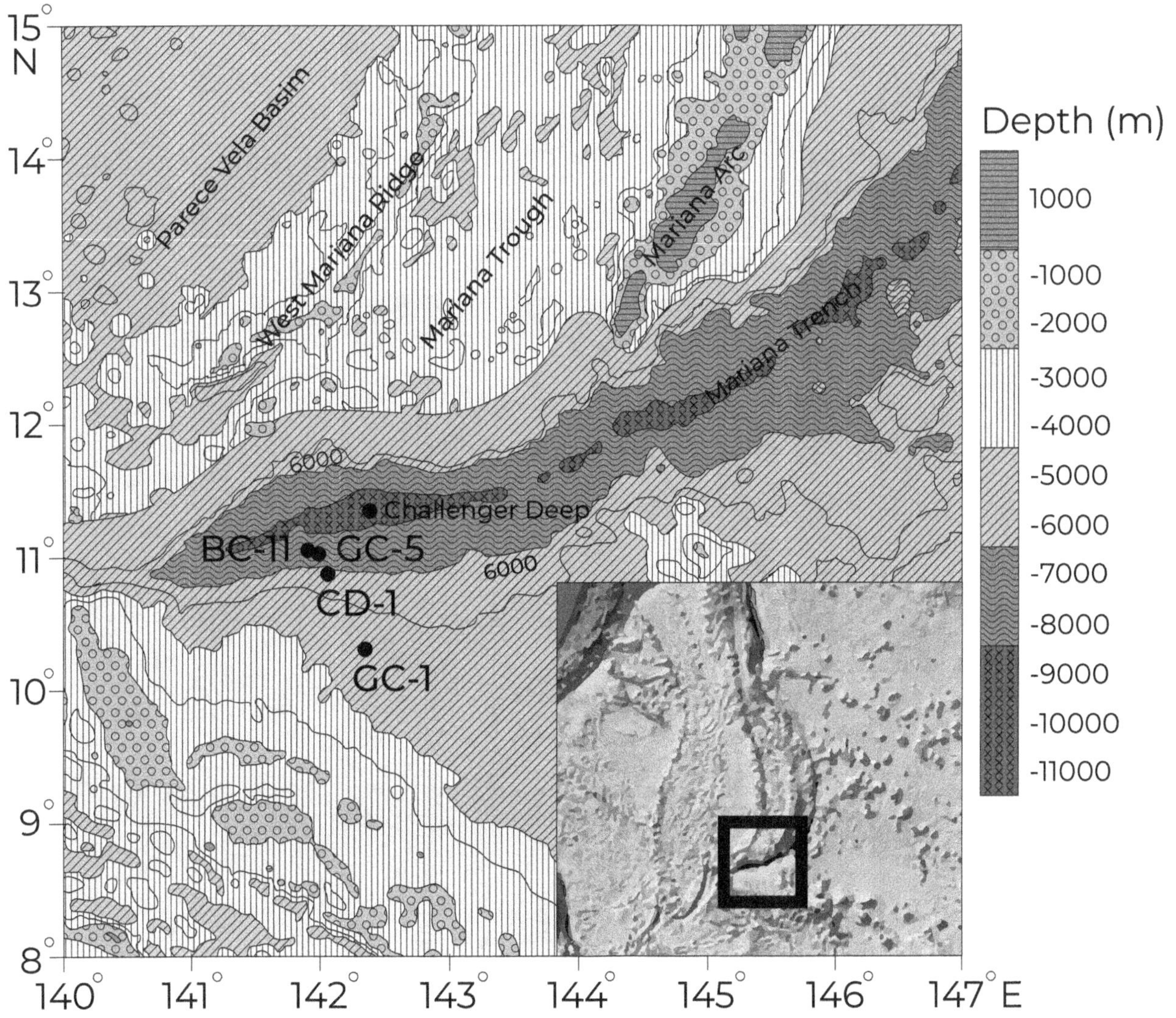

1. Using the color key, how deep is the point Challenger Deep?

2. Describe what an organism living in the Challenger Deep might look like. What types of features would it have and why?

3. What are the two highest areas on the map called?

   A.

   B.

4. Where can living creatures find heat in trenches?

Yesterday you learned about trenches, the deepest parts of our oceans, and the kinds of creatures that live there. Today you will elaborate on the wealth of knowledge about continental drift you've accumulated this week.

Directions: Read and think about each of the questions below, and answer them in complete sentences.

1. Pangaea was surrounded by an ocean called Panthalassa, and during the Paleozoic Era there were shallower oceans. How do you think the life in shallow oceans evolved to be different from the types of life in deep trenches?

....

....

....

....

2. Explain what caused Pangaea to break apart. Use the vocabulary you've learned including continental drift, active plate margins, passive plate margins and trenches.

....

....

....

....

3. The Mid-Atlantic Ridge, a ridge that runs through the center of the Atlantic Ocean the size of the Grand Canyon, is continuing to add new Oceanic Crust to the seafloor at a rate of 1-2 inches per year. Is the Earth going to keep getting bigger? Why or why not?

....

....

....

....

Earth & Space Science

Natural Resources

MS-ESS3-1

Construct a scientific explanation based on evidence for how the uneven distributions of Earth's mineral, energy, and groundwater resources are the result of past and current geoscience processes.

ARGOPREP

Directions: Read the text below. Then answer the questions that follow.

Distribution of Resources

There are certain places that are known for having the best of something. You probably know which place around town has the best pizza and the best sushi. There are also places around the world that are known for having the best or largest quantities of a particular resource. The Middle East is known for its large quantities of oil, the United States for coal, Canada for precious metals, and Brazil for lumber just to name a few. There are all kinds of **Natural Resources** which are materials found around the Earth that can be used by humans. Some natural resources include the air, water, soil, animals, and plants. They also include the minerals, metals, and energy that are mined for wealth and technology. Natural Resources can either be renewable or non-renewable. A **Renewable Resource** is one that may be used but is replaceable in the span of a human lifetime. This can include resources like lumber, livestock, animals, plants, water, sunlight, wind, and air. It is important to note that all of these are only renewable if they are managed properly, since overuse and pollution can quickly turn them to Non-renewable Resources. A Non-renewable Resource is one that is not able to be replaced because it took a very long time to form in the first place, so once it is gone, it cannot be renewed. These are typically things that were formed when the earth first formed billions or hundreds of millions of years ago. Some examples of **Non-renewable Resources** include oil and gas, methane (natural gas), minerals, metals, nuclear power, and coal. These resources are not spread evenly across the world, and their distribution has led to the uneven settling of land around the globe. Wars have broken out over them, entire civilizations have become nomadic for them, and whole countries have ignored a changing climate in their dependency on them.

1. What natural resource is Russia known for?

   A. Coal

   B. Lumber

   C. Oil

   D. Diamonds

2. Give 3 examples of a Renewable Resource:

   A.

   B.

   C.

3. Give 3 examples of a Non-renewable Resource:

   A.

   B.

   C.

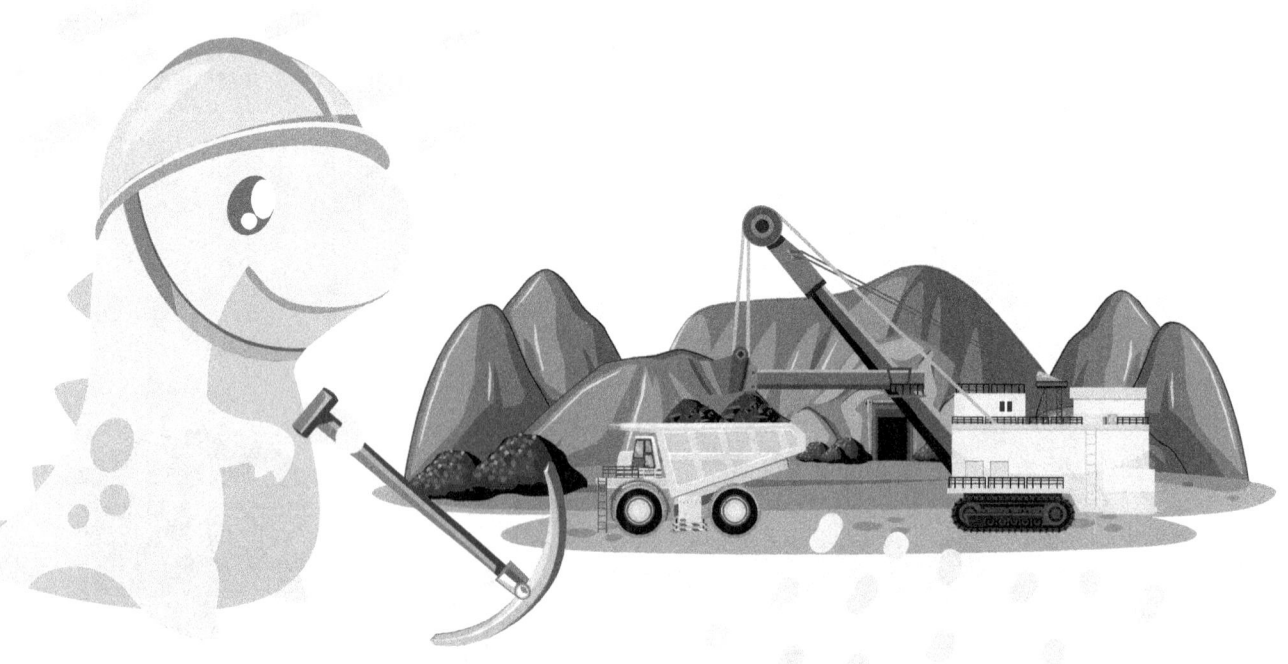

Yesterday you learned about renewable and non-renewable resources around the world. Today you will focus on researching the advantages and disadvantages of different forms of renewable and non-renewable energy.

Directions: Each type of energy has its advantages and disadvantages. Research each energy source to complete the table below.

Natural Resources

Energy Source	Renewable/ Non-renewable	Advantages	Disadvantages	When/ where is the source being utilized?
Solar				
Wind				
Geothermal				
Hydro-power				

Coal				
Oil				
Natural Gas				
Nuclear Power				

Yesterday you completed some research about the different kinds of energy there are as well the advantages and disadvantages of them. Today you will explain which types of resources are best for different reasons.

Directions: Read and answers the questions below.

1. Which types of energy are considered renewable?

2. Which type of renewable resource relies on water?

3. In previous lessons we discussed fossil fuels and climate change. Which resources can lead to pollution and impact climate change in negative ways?

4. Which types of renewable resources would be best for the area you live in? Why?

5. Overall, do renewable resources have more benefits than non-renewable resources?

   A. Yes

   B. No

Yesterday you analyzed the advantages and disadvantages of the different types of resources there are for energy. Today you will think about the region you live in and determine what types of resources are plentiful where you live!

Hometown Natural Resources

Directions: Natural Resources can be either Non-renewable or Renewable, and are unevenly distributed around the globe. Research the state or region where you live, and find out what kinds of resources the place where you live is known for. Draw a picture of the state or area where you live in the space below, and draw and write the kinds of resources found there. For example, if one of the resources your state produces is corn, you could draw an ear of corn. Recall from Day 1 all of the different kinds of resources that are found in nature and how we use them. You may have multiple items, so leave room for all of the great things your home is known for!

Yesterday you drew a map of your home state or region and decorated it with the resources you have access to. Today you will elaborate on your work and draw some conclusions about natural resources in general.

Directions: Read and think about each of the questions below, and answer in complete sentences.

1. What types of renewable resources is your home known for?

2. Since Renewable Resources are dependent on geography and climate, as the climate of the earth changes, how do you think the distribution of Renewable Resources will change with it? Give specific examples of what may be affected.

3. We are in the midst of an energy crisis. We are using up the limited Non-renewable Resources like coal, oil, natural gas, and minerals at a rate that is unsustainable. Soon, they will run out. Do you think using wind, solar, and hydroelectric power could be a good long-term solution to the current energy crisis? Which one do you think is the best option?

4. Freshwater is a Renewable Resource. However, while 70% of the world is covered by water, only 2.5% of that is freshwater and still only 1% of that is drinkable since the rest is trapped in snow and glaciers. What are some factors that can make our freshwater a Non-renewable Resource, and how can we ensure it is protected?

WEEK 16

Engineering
Identifying a Problem

MS-ETS1-1

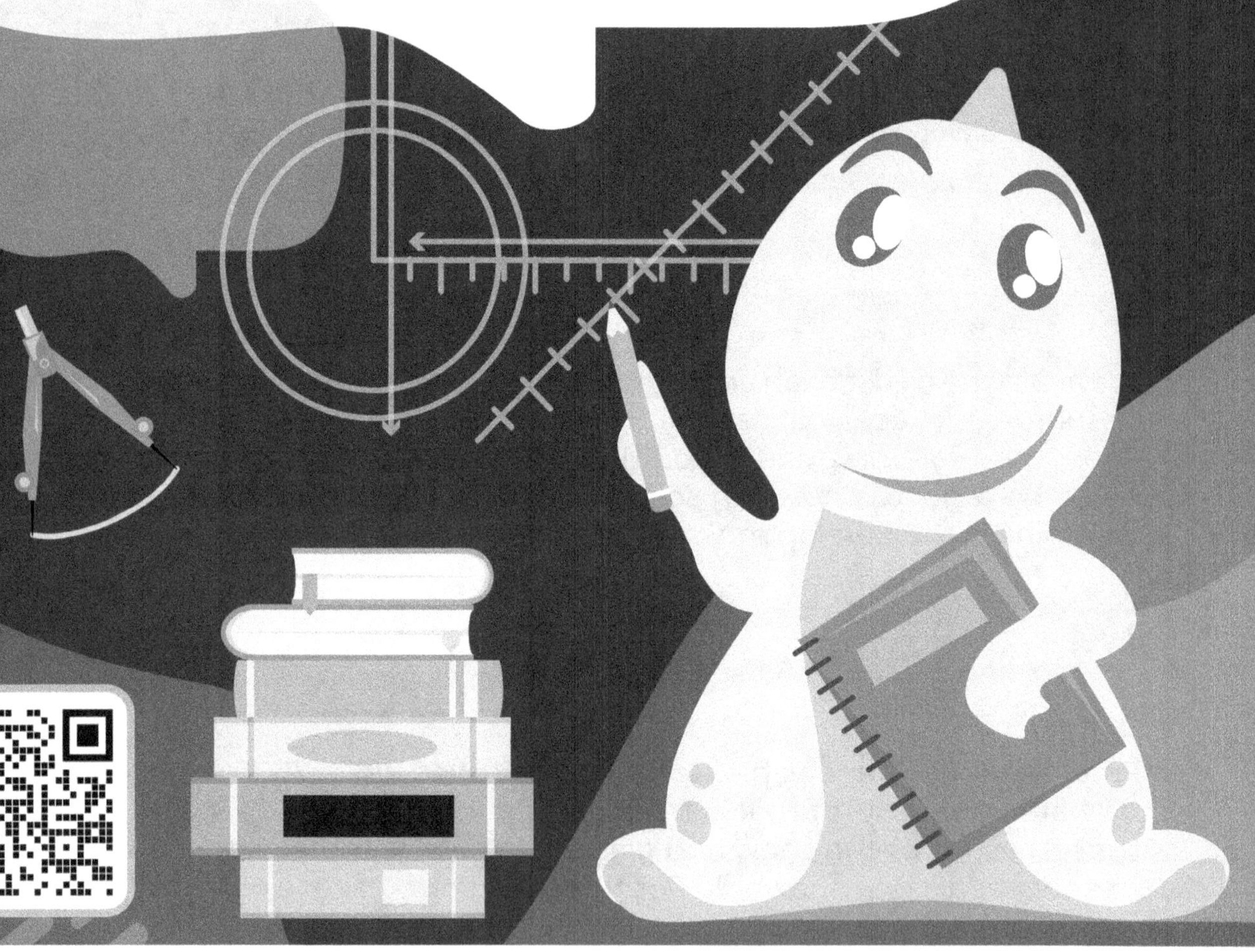

Define the criteria and constraints of a design problem with sufficient precision to ensure a successful solution, taking into account relevant scientific principles and potential impacts on people and the natural environment that may limit possible solutions.

Directions: Read the text below. Then answer the questions that follow.

What is an Engineering Design Spiral?

Engineering is an awesome area of study that combines science, technology, math, and art into one incredible hands-on profession. When beginning an engineering project, it's important to understand the process of engineering. Engineers follow the **Engineering Design Spiral** when they are coming up with a new idea, which allows them to have the best possible finished product at the end. So what is the Engineering Design Spiral? This concept states that all new ideas can continually be improved upon through a spiral process until you reach the center of the spiral where you have achieved the best possible version of that concept.

First, start by identifying a problem that needs a solution. Next, research the problem. Research is important for two reasons: in order to learn more about the problem, and to see what solutions, if any, have already been invented. Sometimes you don't need to come up with a brand new solution, you just need to improve one that already exists. After research comes design. Design is a two-part process where you have to brainstorm all of the ways you could solve the problem you have presented. You can brainstorm ideas by writing them down, sketching them, or both. After you have narrowed your ideas down to a couple of possibilities, you will need to make drafts of them. A draft is a detailed drawing that has very specific information such as measurements. You can even include materials and a budget during this planning phase.

From your drafts you will need to pick the design that solves the problem the best, fits your budget, or is made of the most practical materials. You will then build a prototype of this solution. A **prototype** is a small scale model version of your design that has limited functionality and can be used for testing purposes. It should be made to scale based on your draft but potentially on a smaller scale than your planned design solution depending on what you're trying to build. After the prototyping stage comes testing. This is where the Engineering Design Spiral comes into play because during testing you will continuously need to improve upon your prototype. It is very important to keep good records of every test run so you can go back and see what worked and what didn't in case you need to try something again. In engineering, there are no failures, only opportunities for learning and improving. So if your prototype never works, that's okay. You can simply go back to the spiral and use it as an opportunity to figure out how you can improve upon your design to change your model and try again. Once you have tested and improved your prototype until it's the best it can possibly be, it's time for the last step, building! You will probably need an investor to fund your project, as well as a good marketing team, but you should go out and get your product on the market!

1. What do engineers use to help them come up with new designs?

   A. Drawings

   B. Other people's ideas

   C. Engineering Solution Principle

   D. Engineering Design Spiral

2. Why is Research an important part of the Engineering Design Spiral?

3. What is a small scale model version of your design that has limited functionality called?

   A. Problem

   B. Research

   C. Solution

   D. Prototype

Yesterday you learned how engineers use the Engineering Design Spiral to create solutions to problems. Today you will explore this step-by-step process by completing a diagram in order to visualize it.

Directions: Using what you discovered yesterday about the Engineering Design Spiral, fill in the steps on the spiral below.

Complete the Spiral

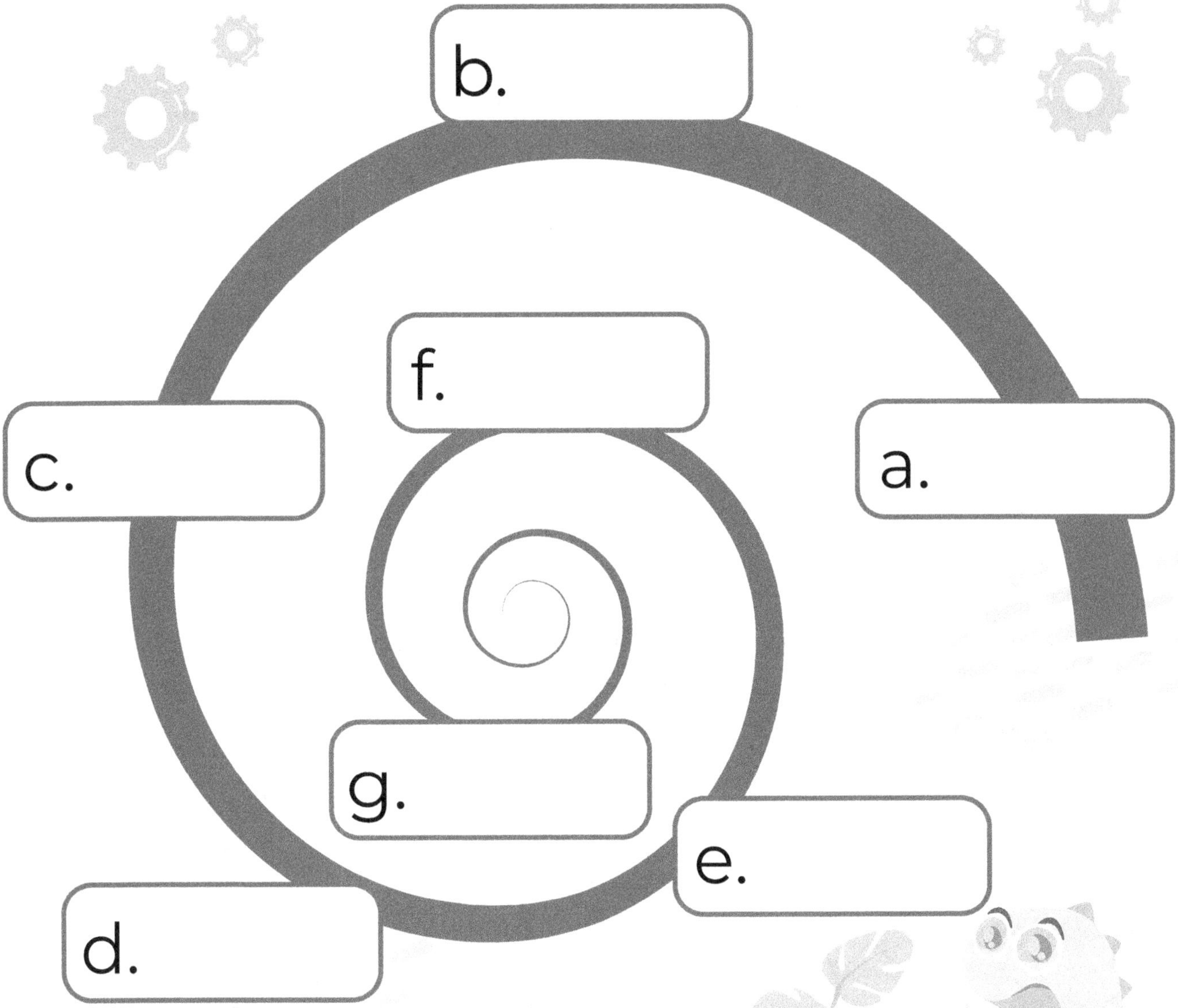

b.

f.

c.

a.

g.

e.

d.

Yesterday you completed a diagram to help you visualize the Engineering Design Spiral. Today you will explain why this process is organized in this particular way and how it helps engineers.

Directions: Read and answer the questions below.

1. Why is it important to start by identifying a problem?

2. What is a budget and why do you need to consider it when creating a solution to a problem?

3. What could happen if you didn't test your solution before selling a product on the market?

4. Let's say I needed to design a bag that was big enough to hold 20 pieces of candy. What could I make in order to test out my design? How would I know if my solution worked?

Yesterday you continued to explain the benefits of using the Engineering Design Spiral. Today you will use this process and identify some problems that arise when designing a rollercoaster, a project you began earlier in this workbook!

Directions: Read each text below. Then answer the questions that follow.

During Week 2 on Day 4, we applied the skills we developed in Physics with Kinetic and Potential Energy and Math with Velocity to design our very own roller coaster. Now you are going to apply those same skills over the next several weeks in an engineering project to build a scale model of a functional roller coaster using the Engineering Design Spiral. If you have another project in mind, you can apply these same design principles to anything. Today, you are going to complete the first step of the spiral which is to identify your problems that could arise when designing a rollercoaster.

Take a moment to think about what kind of roller coaster you would want to build if you could build anything and money was unlimited. Does it have a certain theme? Is there a certain feature or unique design element?

Your roller coaster at a minimum must have:

- One large hill at the beginning that will create Potential Energy to start the Kinetic Energy to get your "vehicle" to the end of the ride
- One loop inversion
- One small hill
- A curve
- Safety rails
- A safe stop at the end of the ride
- A marble for the vehicle
- A construction from simple materials (i.e. - cardboard tubes, paper/card stock, insulator tubing, recycled materials)

1. What are two problems that you could encounter when designing your roller coaster model? Write them below.

2. If your boss wanted you to design a rollercoaster that was also a water ride, do you see any problems that could come from that request?

3. Is it important to start the Design Spiral by identifying potential problems?

   A. Yes
   B. No

Yesterday you identified some possible problems that could arise when designing your rollercoaster and building a model. Today you will elaborate on these problems and consider how you will create solutions to them.

Directions: Read and answer the questions below.

1. Did you find any problems with your initial roller coaster design?

   A. Yes

   B. No

2. Look back at question #1 from yesterday. What are two possible solutions to one of the problems you identified?

   ....

   ....

   ....

3. What is one part of your design that you really like so far and why?

   ....

   ....

   ....

   ....

   ....

   ....

4. If an engineer designed a rollercoaster without considering problems first, what could happen?

   ....

   ....

   ....

   ....

Engineering

Developing a Solution

MS-ETS1-2

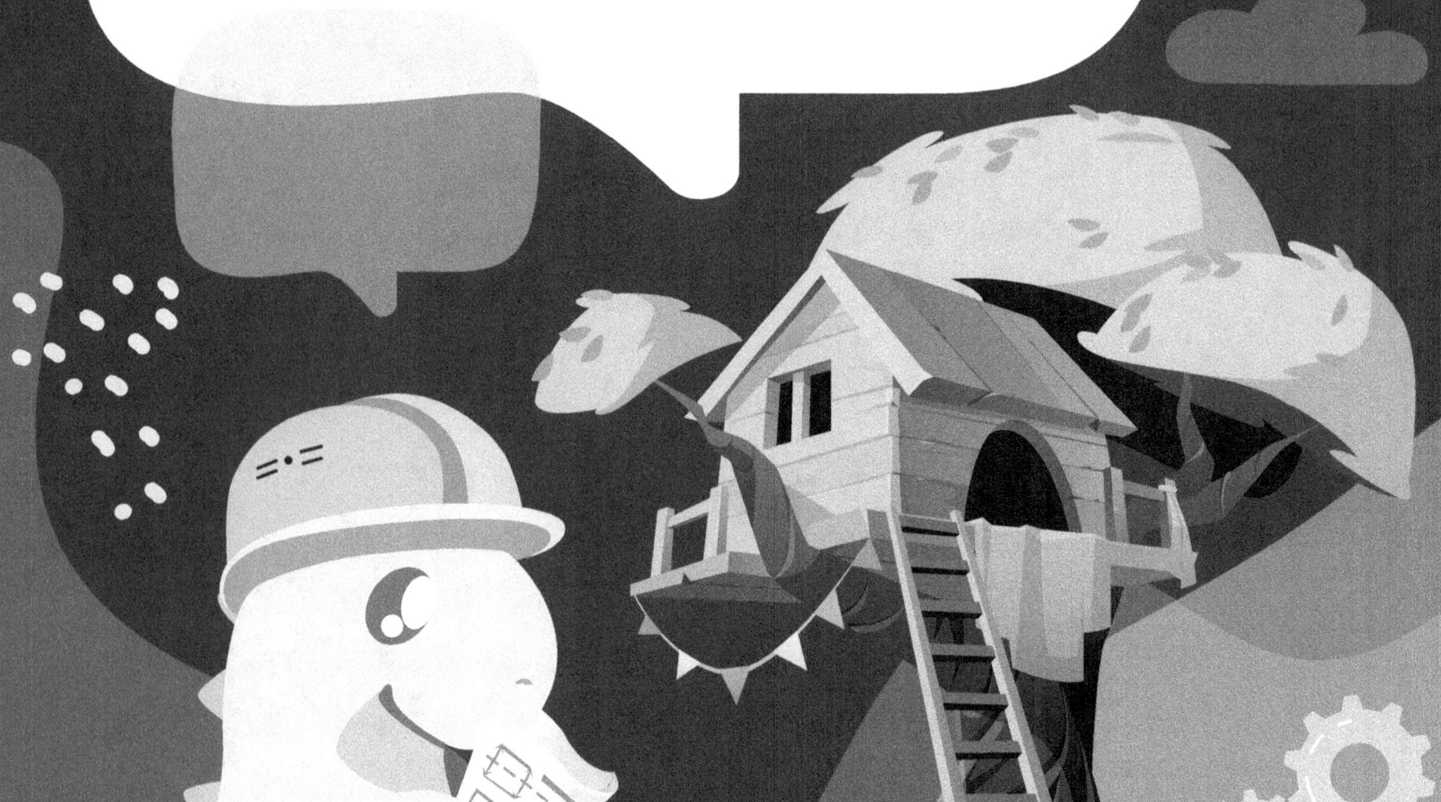

Evaluate competing design solutions using a systematic process to determine how well they meet the criteria and constraints of the problem.

ARGOPREP

Directions: Read the text below. Then answer the questions that follow.

How to Solve a Problem

Now that you have come up with some potential problems to solve through engineering—a discipline that combines innovation and imagination with data to create new technologies—you can use your research to decide on possible solutions. These solutions can be written out or displayed as rough sketches. Next, you will need to create multiple rough sketches of your idea from different angles: front view, side view, and top-down view. This ensures you are considering all important angles and parts of your design in three dimensions. What's the difference between a rough sketch and final draft? A rough sketch is not to scale and does not necessarily have straight lines or perfect angles. It is a simple, quick way to get ideas out of your head and onto paper. A final draft is to scale and uses a scale rule on graph paper or is made on a computer.

What does it mean to draw your final draft "**to scale**"? If your final product is actually 20 feet long, you will want to have a drawing where 1 foot = $\frac{1}{2}$ inch. This way, your drawing will only be a total of 10 inches long. However, using a scale rule will make translating the draft to a full size product simple since the entire ruler is scaled down so that every $\frac{1}{2}$" of actual measurement is equal to 1' of measurement on the ruler. This is the way that model boats and model cars are made, with original plans drawn to scale. If you'd like to try computerized 3D drawing as a beginner, as of this writing, SketchUp is a great way to start; it has a free program and is intuitively user friendly. You can also create a 3D print from SketchUp if that is an option for you.

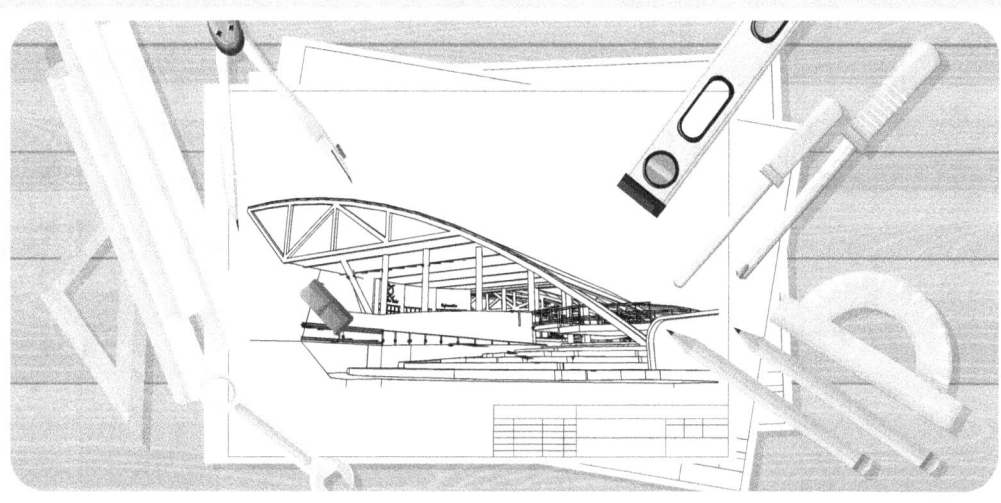

1. How many views do you need to draw your sketches from?

   A. 1

   C. 3

   B. 2

   D. 4

2. What's the difference between a rough sketch and a final draft?

3. True/False: Final drafts don't need to include measurements.

   A. True

   B. False

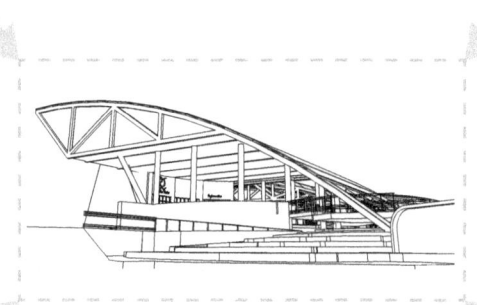

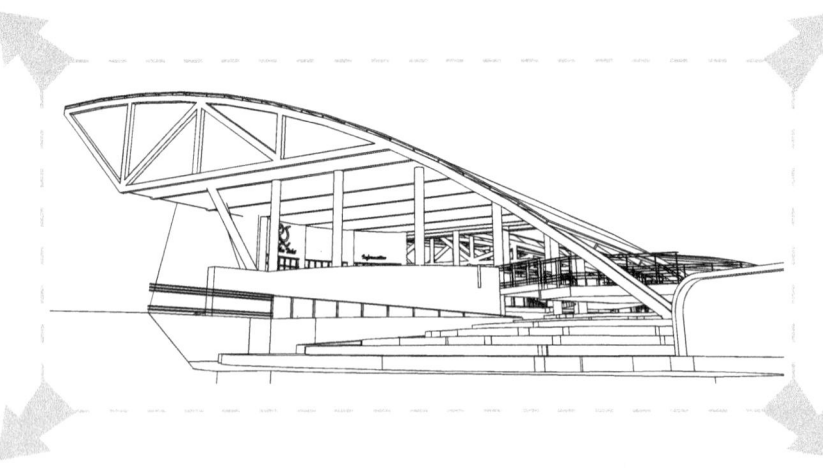

Yesterday you learned about the importance of drawing a rough draft of an idea or a solution to a problem. Today you will practice designing a treehouse and drawing a draft of it to scale.

Directions: Using the graph paper below, draw an image to scale following the specifications.

Design a Treehouse to Scale

Practice drawing to scale: You have been tasked with designing the ultimate treehouse. The dimensions for the backyard treehouse must be no larger than 7 feet tall x 9 feet wide to fit in the space of the tree. The graph paper scale is 1 foot = 2 units. The graph paper below is 20 units x 20 units. Design an ultimate treehouse that is within the maximum size limit and that is awesome!

1. What are the maximum dimensions of your treehouse in units? How many units tall by units wide does your treehouse measure on the graph?

.... units tall x .... units wide

2. How do these dimensions translate into feet? How big is your treehouse in feet?

.... feet tall x .... feet wide

Yesterday you practiced drawing a treehouse to scale. Today you will explain how this relates to your work designing a rollercoaster.

Directions: Read the information below and sketch your rollercoaster. Then answer the questions that follow.

Creating a Rough Draft

Last week, you were tasked with beginning an engineering project to design a new roller coaster. This week, you will take your ideas and background research that you worked on last week and draw a rough draft of your ideas using the graph paper below. Today, draw a draft of only the front view of your roller coaster. It is important to determine the scale at which you are drawing it, just like you did with the treehouse yesterday.

Remember to include the minimum requirements from last week for your roller coaster - some of these will be very important when you build your 3D model:

1. One large hill at the beginning that will create Potential Energy to start the Kinetic Energy to get your "vehicle" to the end of the ride
2. One loop inversion
3. One small hill
4. A curve
5. Safety rails
6. A safe stop at the end of the ride
7. A marble for the vehicle

```
   0   1   2   3   4   5   6   7   8   9  10  11  12  13  14  15  16  17  18  19  20  21  22  23  24  25  26  27  28  29  30
 1
 2
 3
 4
 5
 6
 7
 8
 9
10
11
12
13
14
15
16
17
18
19
20
```

1. What is the tallest point on your rollercoaster in feet and/or inches? This is how tall it would actually be if you built it.

2. How tall is the tallest point in your drawing in units? This is asking how you drew your draft "to scale."

3. How long is your rollercoaster in graph paper units?

Yesterday you drew a scale draft of your rollercoaster looking at it from the front. Today you will draw a top-down and a side view draft and continue to think about how to scale your models.

Directions: Read the following and then complete the two new drawings.

Today, you will sketch the other two views of your rough draft: top-down and side view. These other views will help you get a three-dimensional perspective of what the finished product will look like and will help you later when you need to refer back to what you were first imagining.

Top-Down Rough Draft

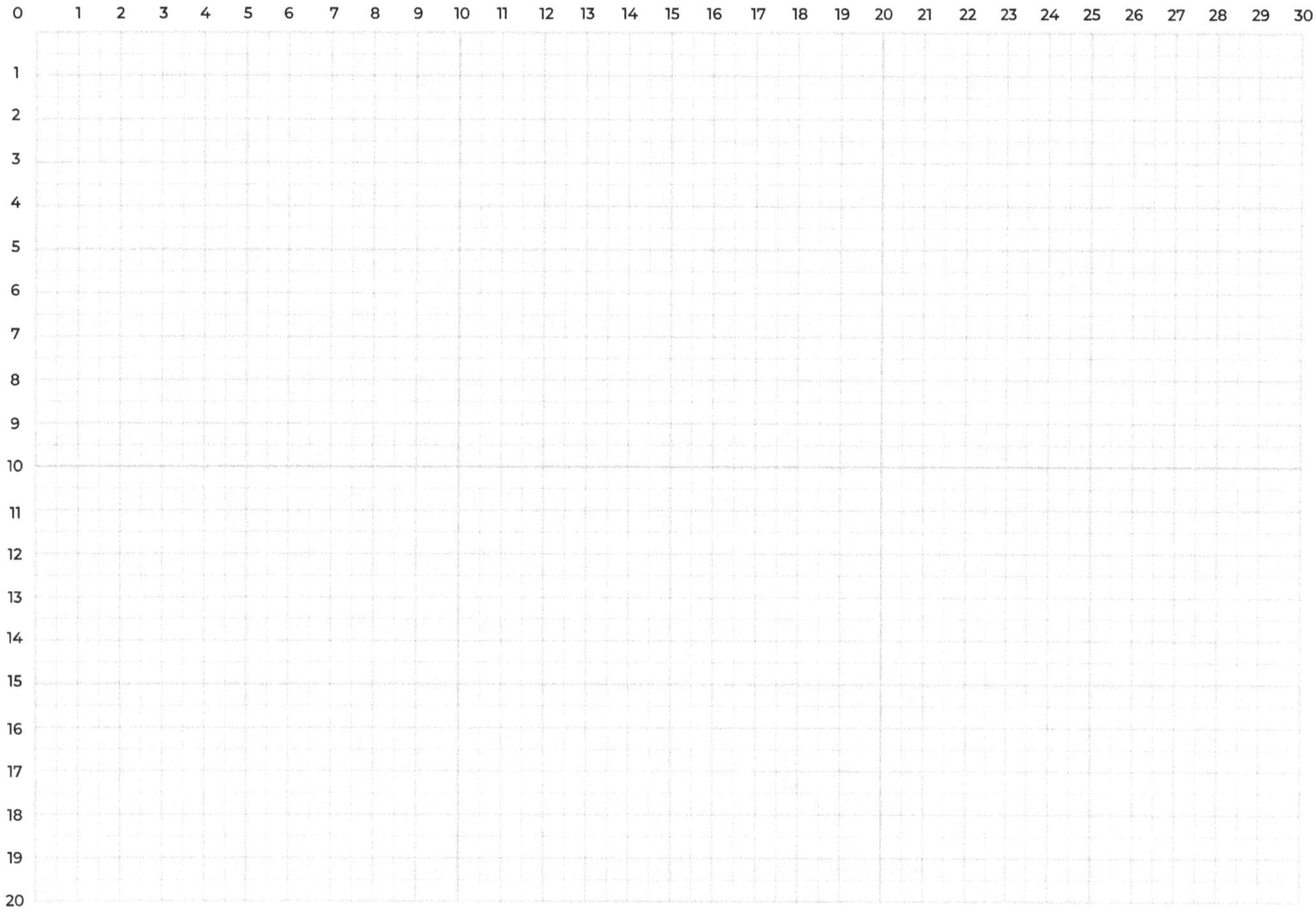

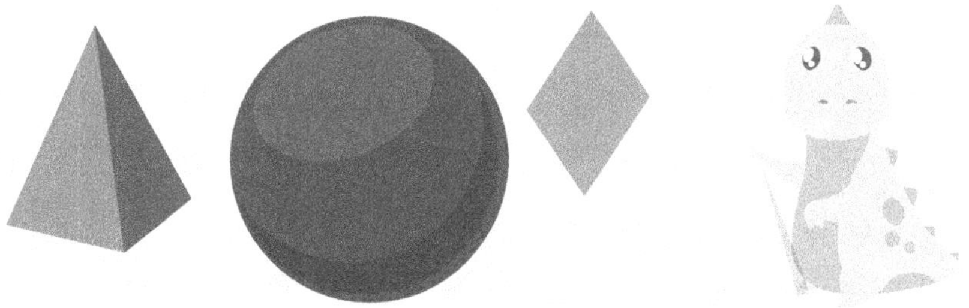

Side View Rough Draft

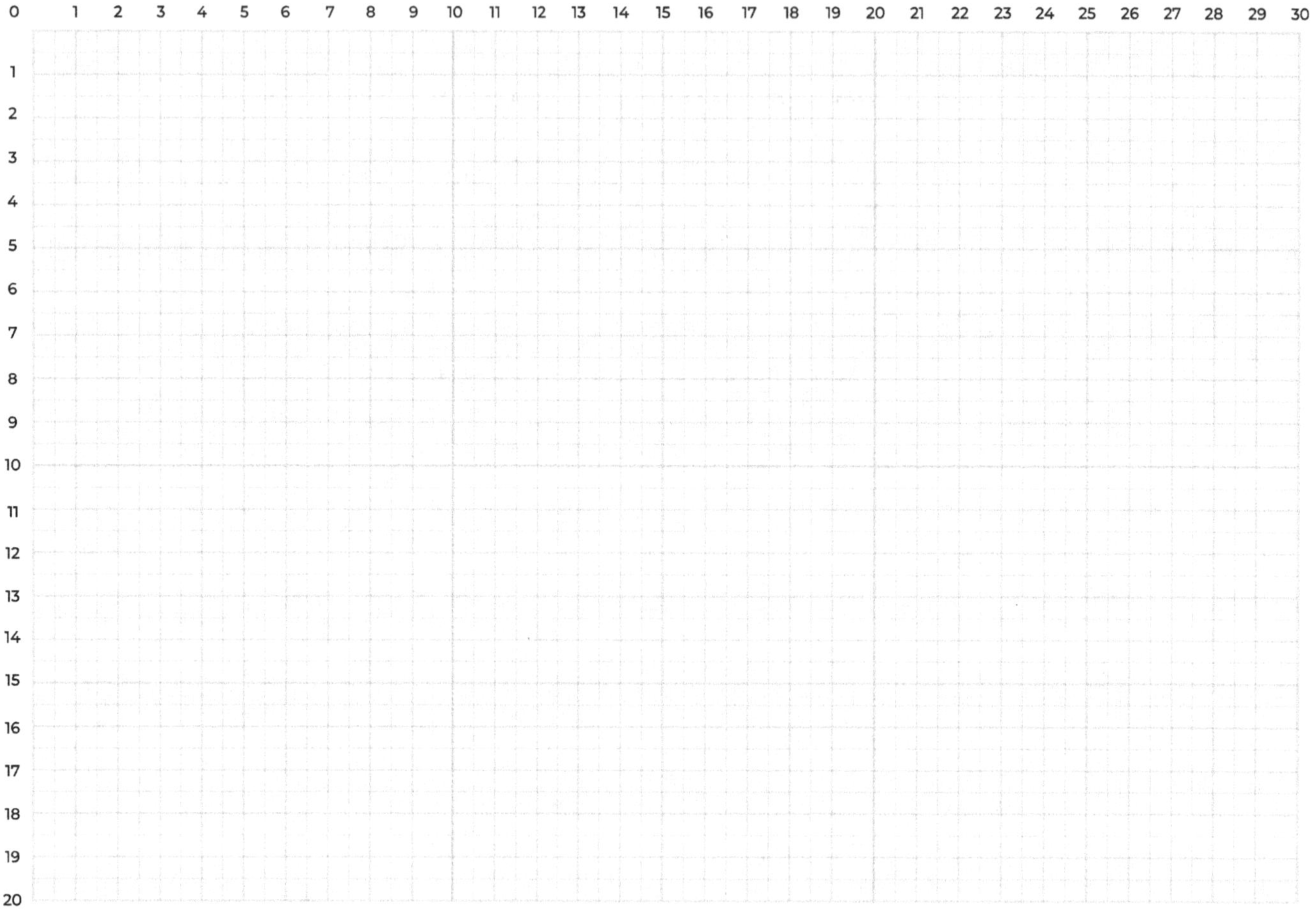

	1	2	3	4	5	6	7	8	9	10	11	12	13	14	15	16	17	18	19	20	21	22	23	24	25	26	27	28	29	30
1																														
2																														
3																														
4																														
5																														
6																														
7																														
8																														
9																														
10																														
11																														
12																														
13																														
14																														
15																														
16																														
17																														
18																														
19																														
20																														

Directions: Answer each of the following questions based on what you have discovered this week about sketching rough drafts.

1. Which view did you find was the easiest to visualize and draw?

   A. Front View

   B. Top-Down View

   C. Side View

2. Which view do you think was the hardest to visualize and draw?

   A. Front View

   B. Top-Down View

   C. Side View

3. Why do you think certain views were easier or more difficult to visualize and sketch out?

   ....

   ....

   ....

4. Did the scale change between your front view and top-down drawings?

   A. Yes

   B. No

5. What do you think are the benefits of having a rough draft before you make the final draft?

   ....

   ....

   ....

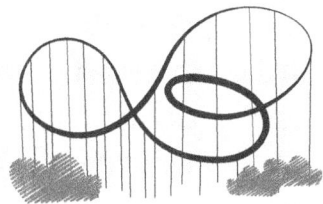

Engineering

Drafting and Redesigning Based on Data

MS-ETS1-3

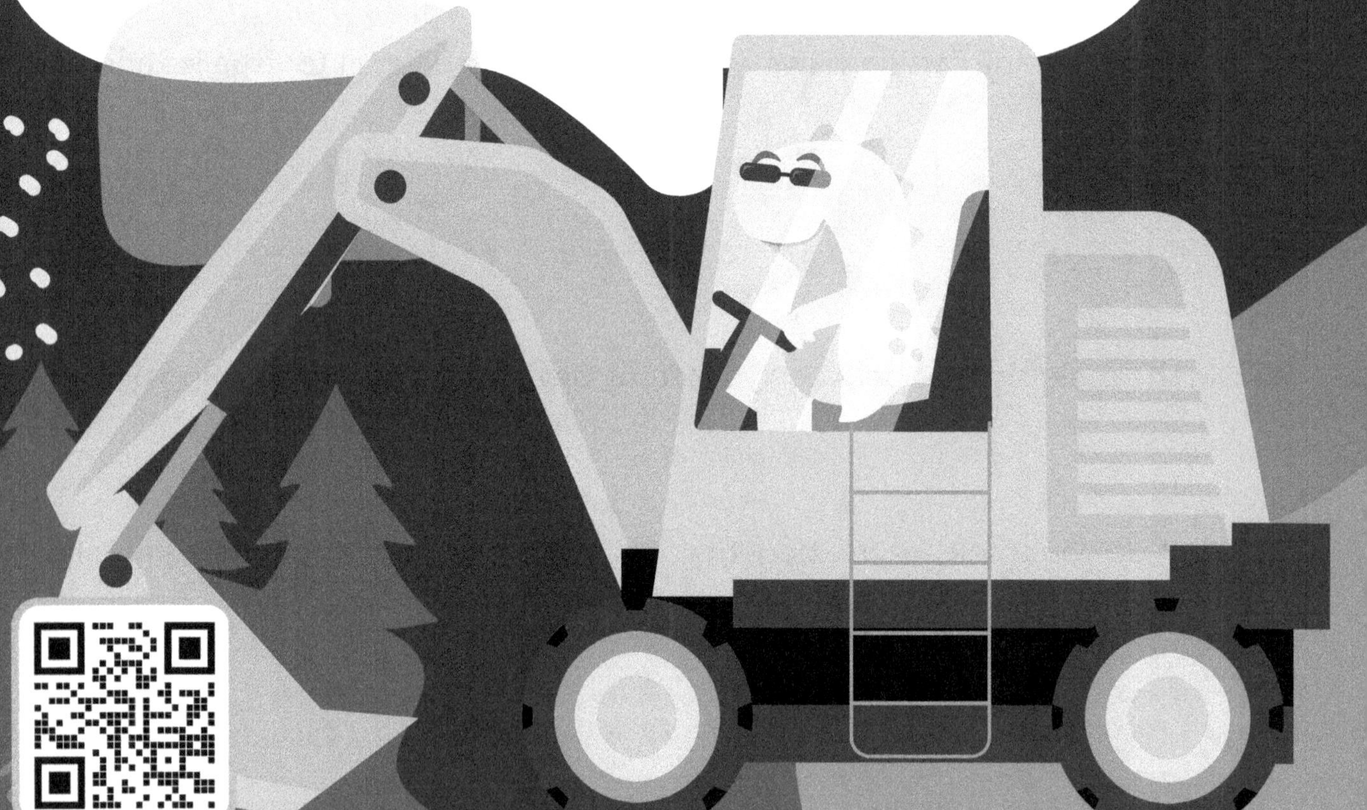

Analyze data from tests to determine similarities and differences between several design solutions. Identify the best characteristics of each that can be combined into a new solution to better meet the criteria for success.

Directions: Read the text below. Then answer the questions that follow.

Creating a Final Draft On A Computer

Last week, you created a rough draft of your rollercoaster in three dimensions. This week, you will be finalizing your rough draft sketches in order to create your Final Draft of all three dimensions. This can be done on graph paper or by using a CAD (Computer Assisted Design) program, like AutoCad or SketchUp. Your Final Draft must be done with straight edges using a ruler, exact curves, and precise measurements. Having measurements on your final draft will make it easier to build your model next. It should be drawn to scale, meaning you know what measurements on your drawing are equal to 1 foot in full scale. When drawing using CAD, your drawing will include the actual measurements and will be scaled for you. It makes the process much easier, but it can be a little time consuming when you are first figuring out the program. If you were building something small, drawing to scale wouldn't be necessary because you would just draw to the actual size.

1. What are two ways you can make a Final Draft?

   A. ....

   B. ....

2. What does a final draft need that a rough draft did not have?

   A. Straight Edges

   B. Detailed Measurements

   C. Exact Curves

   D. All of the above

3. Why are measurements important on a Final Draft?

   A. To show off to others

   B. To take extra time

   C. To build the final product

   D. To practice your measuring and math skills

Yesterday you learned why it is so important to use a computer to create final drafts of your ideas. Today you will practice designing a new product so you can later translate your idea to a computer model.

Directions: Using the graph paper below, draw an image to scale following the specifications.

Invent a Pooper Scooper to Scale

You have been tasked with inventing a mechanism to pick up dog waste that is simpler for people with a limited range of motion and have a service dog. The pooper scooper can be robotic or manual. The dimensions for it should be no larger than 3 feet x 3 feet. The graph paper scale is 1 foot = 5 units. The graph paper below is 20 units x 20 units. Design an amazing new pooper scooper that will help this population, that is within the maximum size limit, and that could be functional. You will need to include actual measurements for length, width, and height. Then, using a CAD program, try to translate your drawn model to a computer model.

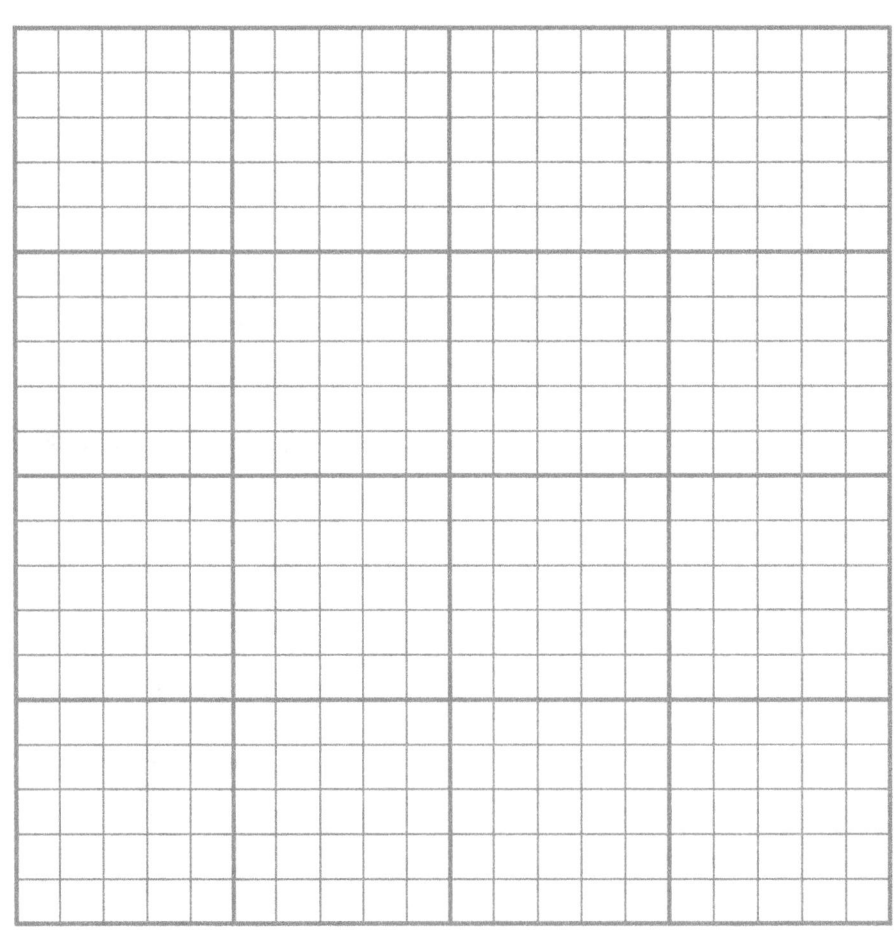

1. What are the maximum dimensions of your pooper scooper in units? How many units tall by units wide does your device measure on the graph?

   .... units tall x .... units wide

2. How do these dimensions translate into feet? How big is your pooper scooper in feet?

   .... feet tall x .... feet wide

3. Was it easy or hard to learn how to use the CAD program?

   A. Easy

   B. Difficult

4. What was one benefit of using the computer program?

Yesterday you practiced taking a design idea and translating it to a CAD program. Today you will complete a similar process with your roller coaster design.

Directions: Read each text below. Then answer the questions that follow.

Creating a Final Draft

Last week, you were tasked with creating your rough draft from the Engineering project that had you design a new roller coaster. This week, you will take your ideas and background research you worked on previously plus the rough draft from last week, and you'll draw a final draft of your ideas using the graph paper below. Remember your final draft must include exact dimensions and measurements. Today draw only the front view of your roller coaster on the graph paper below, or using CAD if you wish. Use a ruler, protractor or another curved object to help you. Be sure to write

the scale below the graph to help you remember the size of your measurements. For example, 1 foot = $\frac{1}{4}$ inch, or 1 foot = 1 unit block. You may find that your rough

draft needs adjustments as you create your final draft, and that's okay. Being able to make improvements is part of the Engineering Design Spiral. Once you have your CAD drawing, you can print it and tape it here in this workbook.

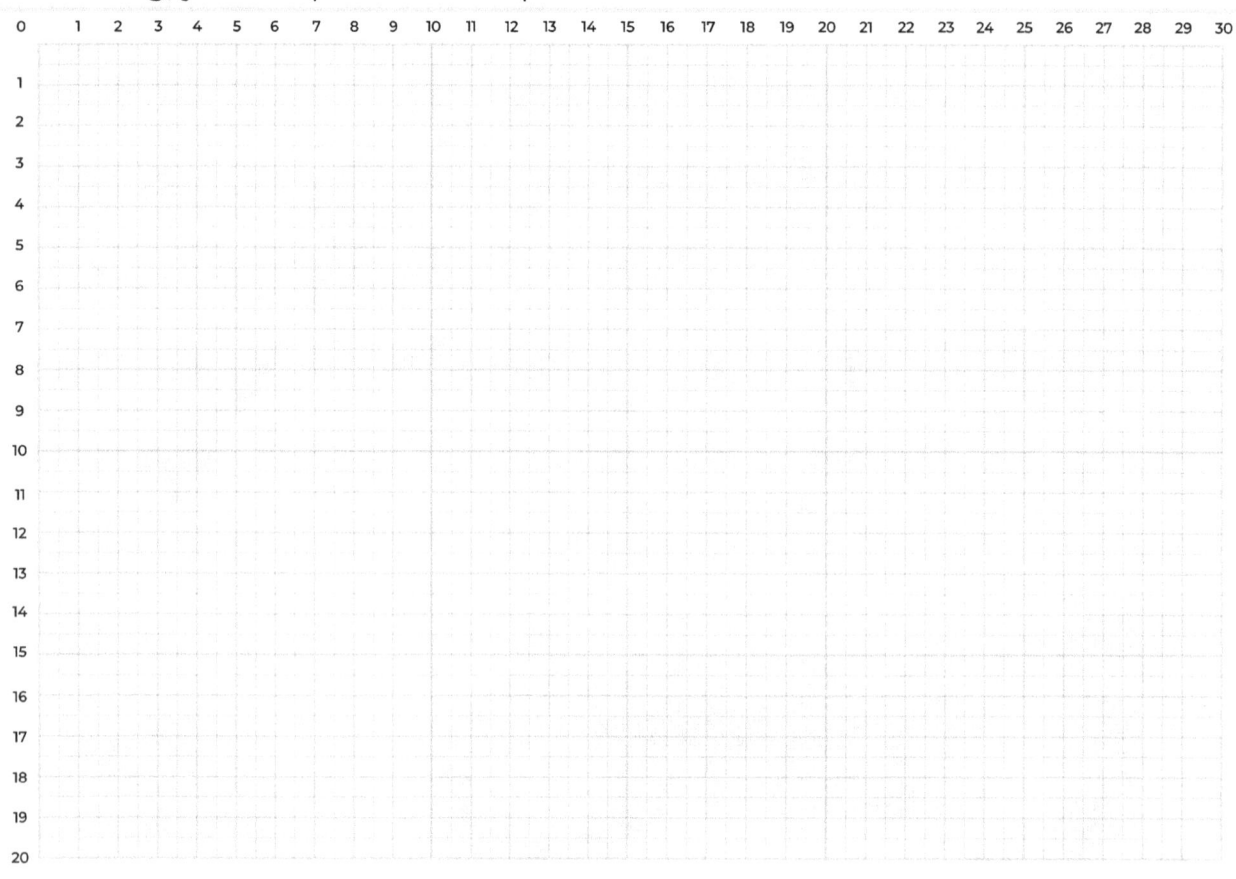

Yesterday you used CAD in order to create a scale model of your rollercoaster. Today you will complete the same process, except this time you will focus on translating your top-down and side view drawings to CAD.

Today, you will draw the other two views of your Final Draft: top-down and side view. These other views will help you get a three-dimensional perspective of what the finished product will look like when it is built. They will also help you later when you need to refer back to what you were first imagining. The ability to imagine shapes in three dimensions and to draw images in three dimensions on a two-dimensional surface is called **Orthographic Drawing**. This can also be done using a CAD program without drawing three separate drawings, since it automatically is in the three-dimensional space. Once you are done, print out your scale CAD drawings and paste them in this workbook.

Top-Down Final Draft

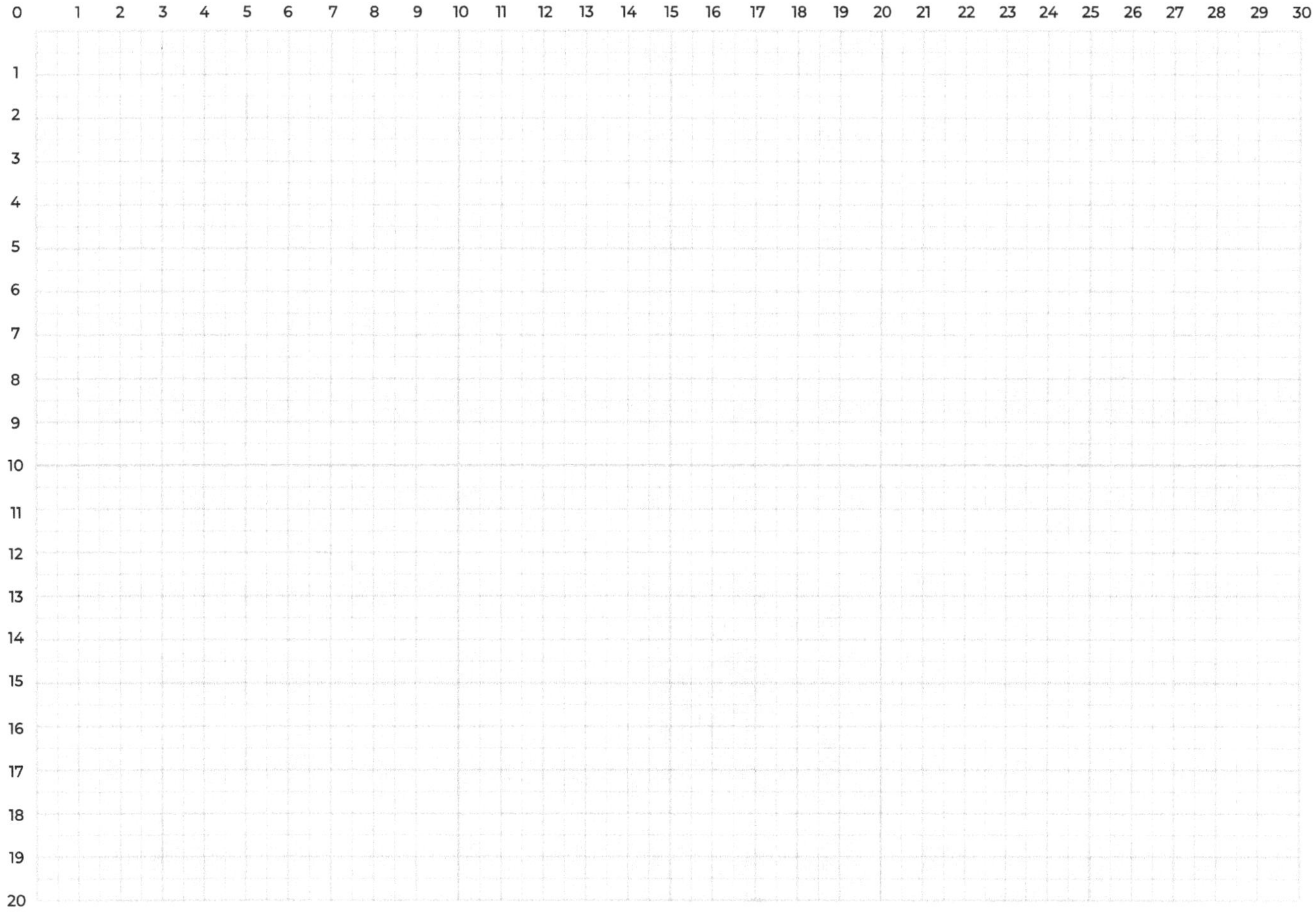

Side View Final Draft

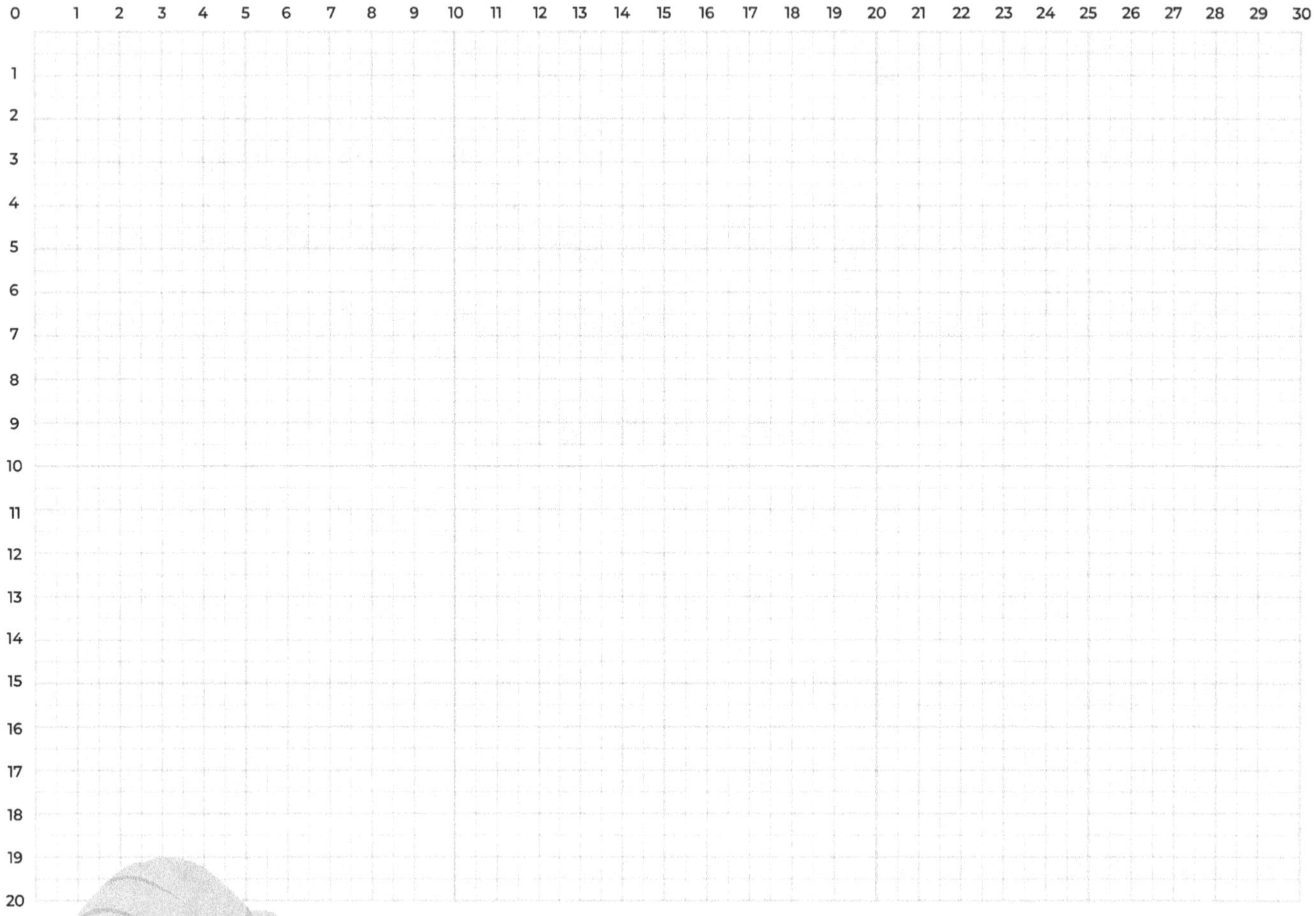

Yesterday you completed two orthographic drawings of your roller coaster on a CAD program. Today you will elaborate on that process and discuss how it went.

Directions: Answer each of the following based on what you have discovered this week about drawing final drafts and Orthographic Drawing.

1. How did drawing a final draft on CAD with measurements differ from sketching a rough draft?

2. Did you change anything from your original idea to your rough draft to your final draft? If so, why?

3. Would you use this method again for designing a new concept? Why or why not?

Engineering

Developing a Model and Testing

MS-ETS1-4

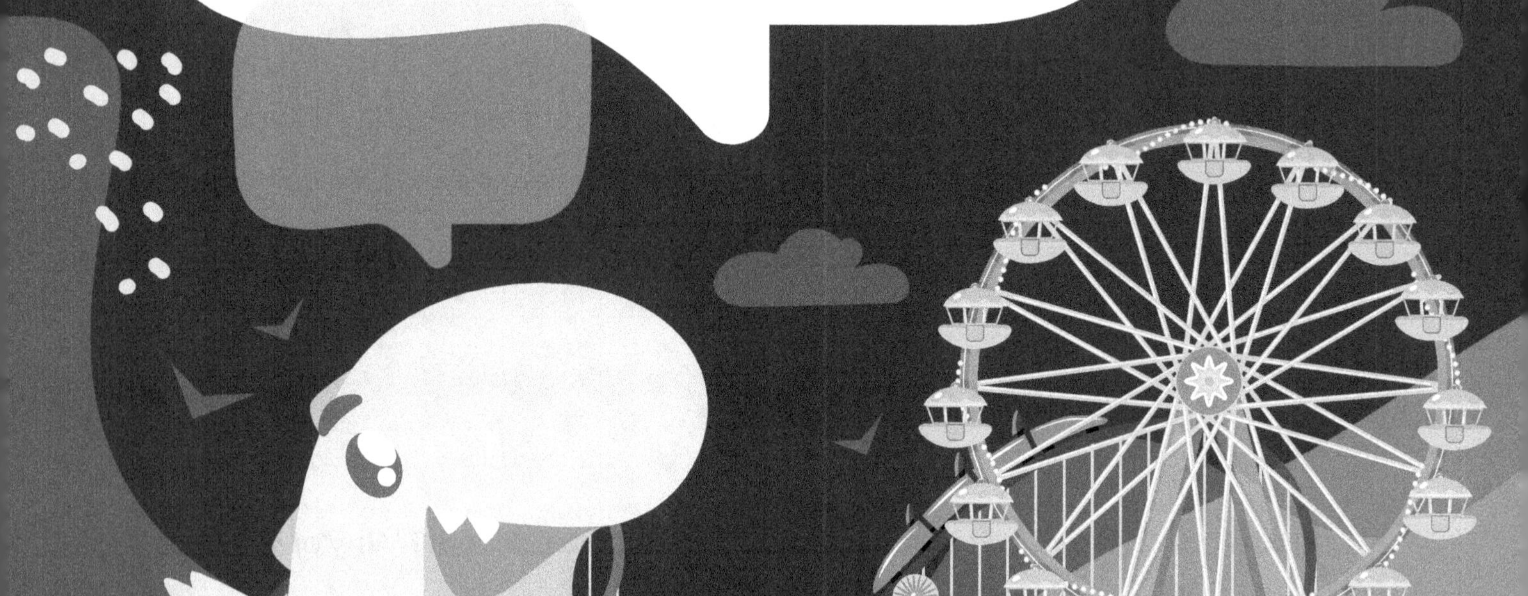

Develop a model to generate data for iterative testing and modification of a proposed object, tool, or process such that an optimal design can be achieved.

Directions: Read the text below. Then answer the questions that follow.

How to Build a Model

Once you have decided what you are building, completed your research, and finished your rough sketches and final drafts, it's time to build a model. Constructing a physical object helps bring your ideas to life. This important stage is also critical in the Engineering Design Spiral to help you test your idea and determine what works and what needs to be adjusted. By building a model that has limited functionality, you are able to complete multiple test runs and fix anything that doesn't work. So how do you actually build a model from your final draft?

Start by deciding how big you want to build your model. It can be as big or as small as you want. Use the measurements in your final draft to scale your model up or down to the size you planned. For example, if you planned for 1 inch = 1 foot, but you wanted to build a model that is bigger than your draft and smaller than your finished product, then you could make a model that is 2 inch = 1 inch scale in the drawing. Next, you should decide what materials you will use to build your model. It can be made out of found objects, recycled materials, or items specifically purchased for this purpose. The final step is to have fun building it! It's okay if it doesn't work at first. It's important not to get frustrated in these early stages but to let your creativity come through. During testing, you can make adjustments to help the model become more functional when solving your initial problem.

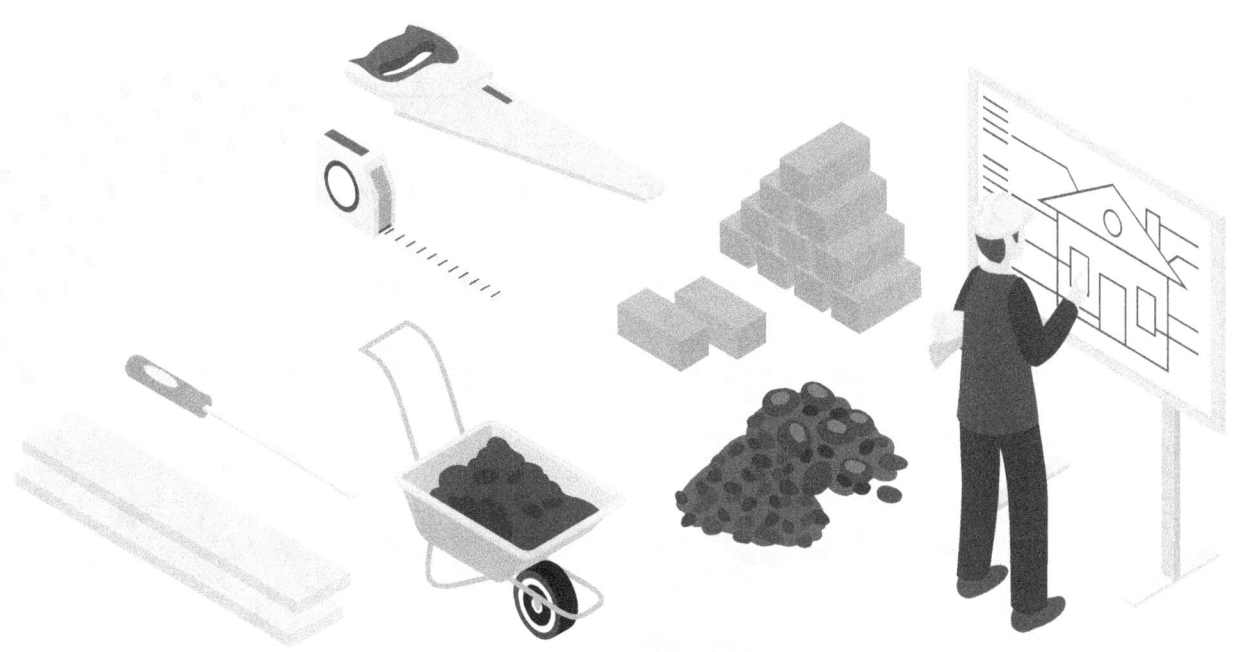

1. Why is it important to build a model?

   A. It's fun
   B. To get funding for the final project
   C. To help you test your idea, figure out what works, and change what doesn't
   D. To show off your idea

2. Explain how you can use your measurements to build a model to scale.

3. What kinds of materials can you build a model out of?

   A. Recycled toilet paper tubes, paper towel tubes, soda cans...
   B. Old CDs, cardboard box, pencils...
   C. Foam insulator tubing, dowels, paint...
   D. All of the above

Yesterday you learned about the importance of making a 3D model of your design based on your drawn drafts. Today you will explore this process by trying to make a 3D model of your rollercoaster!

Directions: Read each text below. Then answer the questions that follow.

For the last two weeks, you have been tasked with coming up with some amazing new concepts. Today you will begin working on your roller coaster model you have spent time conceptualizing, researching, drafting, and redrafting. Remember that it must follow certain criteria:

- One large hill at the beginning that will create Potential Energy to start the Kinetic Energy to get your "vehicle" to the end of the ride
- One loop inversion
- One small hill
- A curve
- Safety rails
- A safe stop at the end of the ride
- A marble for the vehicle

The model can be made from recycled materials, found objects, or anything you want. Use your scale drawings to create this 3D model that will help you better envision your idea. It must be functional and use gravity and kinetic energy for power. Expect your construction to take some time. When you are finished for today, answer the following questions.

1. How closely does your model match your original design plans?

2. What materials are you making your model out of? Why did you choose these materials?

3. Explain your process for building your model. Where did you decide to start?

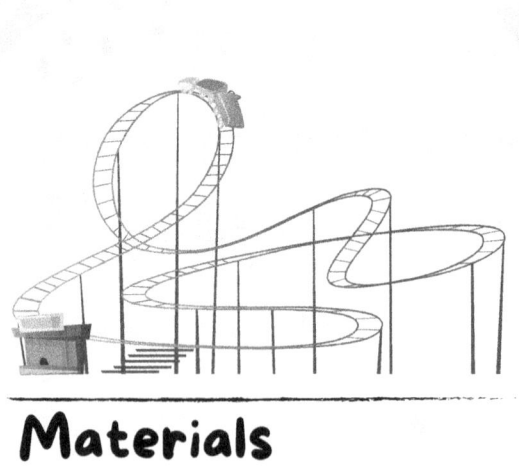

Materials

Yesterday you began creating a 3D model of your rollercoaster based on your final draft drawings. Today you will spend some time analyzing how the build is going and what you could do to improve your model.

Directions: Read each text below. Then answer the questions that follow.

The Iterative Process

Today, you will continue working on your roller coaster model. Building a model takes time. You are now in the "**iterative process**" of the Engineering Design Spiral. The iterative process is the method of repeating an action over and over again to get closer and closer to the desired result. By spending more time working on your model, you are getting it closer to where it needs to be in the end. There is always something better that can be done and some new improvement to be made. As Walt Disney once said, "Whenever I go on a ride, I'm always thinking of what's wrong with the thing and how it can be improved." While you are building your roller coaster, you can begin testing components. You don't even need to wait for it to be completed to start running tests. We will discuss testing more in depth tomorrow.

1. Explain the iterative process and how it will help you have a better product.

2. How much farther did you get in your model building today?

3. Is it going the way you expected, or are you experiencing some difficulty?

Yesterday you finished building your first 3D model of your rollercoaster after considering what changes you might need to make to it. Today you will test your model in order to obtain more data about how it functions.

Testing your Roller Coaster Model

Today you will begin using a testing log sheet to help you keep track of your tests as you build in the Engineering Design Spiral. During each step of your building process, you will be running tests to figure out how well the roller coaster is working. Does the loop actually work? Is the hill high enough to create the energy needed to get it around the loop and over the hill? Are the curves protected so that the marble doesn't fall off the edge? Mark down what happens during each test and what changes you made to fix problems. Expect to have many more unsuccessful trials than successful ones. Don't get discouraged; this is normal. Keep trying!

Test #	Successful/ Unsuccessful	Why? How will you fix it?

Test #	Successful/ Unsuccessful	Why? How will you fix it?

Yesterday you tested your roller coaster model and recorded some observations about it. Today you will consider what redesigns you might need to make on your model so that it is an even better design in the end.

Directions: Read and answer each question below.

Redesigning your Model

Now that you are on the right track building your model and have begun testing, it is time to continue with the iterative process and redesign your model. It is important to keep improving so you can move toward the best possible product. Your roller coaster should be functional so your marble rolls from the top of the hill, around the loop, and safely stops at the end. You will know it is completely functional when the marble completes its run every time. Continued improvements can be made by adding artistic elements like your theme embellishments with paint, landscaping, and graphic design.

1. Was the marble able to travel the entire length of the rollercoaster?

   A. Yes

   B. No

2. What is something you might need to add to your model to make it function better?

   ....

   ....

   ....

3. What is something that is working very well with your model currently?

   ....

   ....

   ....

4. Do you see how testing the model allows you to determine ways to redesign it and improve it?

   A. Yes

   B. No

WEEK 20

Engineering
Evaluating, Redesigning, and Modifying

MS-ETS1-4

Develop a model to generate data for iterative testing and modification of a proposed object, tool, or process such that an optimal design can be achieved.

ARGOPREP

Directions: Read the text below. Then answer the questions that follow.

Designing On A Budget

For the past four weeks, you have been using the Engineering Design Spiral to create a model of a rollercoaster. This week we will discuss what it would look like if we were to take your 3D model at a real theme park. One thing we discussed briefly in Week 15 was budget. Most businesses do not have an unlimited amount of money in order to make a product. Instead, they have a budget that marks the maximum amount they can spend. This is called a **constraint**. Constraints aren't necessarily a bad thing. In fact, they often force engineers to think of solutions in new and creative ways. Other constraints include time and safety. For example, you could probably build a pretty wild rollercoaster if you didn't care much about safety, but since people are riding it, there are certain things you must consider in terms of safety.

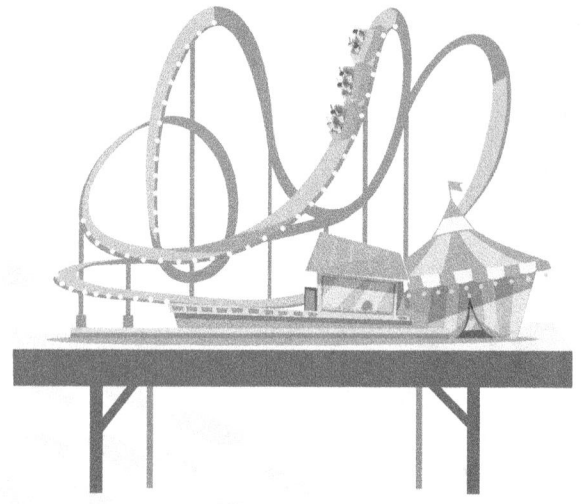

1. Which of these is not a constraint?

   A. Time

   B. Modeling

   C. Budget

   D. Safety

2. Are constraints a bad thing?

   A. Yes

   B. No

3. Which of these would be a way to make sure a project was within a budget?

   A. Add up the cost of the materials and make sure it is more than the budget

   B. Just build the product and see what happens

   C. Add up the cost of the materials and make sure it is less than the budget

   D. Ask someone else to do it

Yesterday you learned about constraints that can affect engineers when designing a solution to a problem. Today you will explore how to work within certain constraints.

Directions: Read the text below. Then answer the questions that follow.

Timory is planting a garden for her mother and wants to make sure it has all of her favorite vegetables in it. She has $18 to spend on plants at the nursery. Her mother's favorites are rutabagas, spinach, cucumbers, tomatoes and black-eyed peas. When Timory arrives at the nursery, she takes note of all of the prices of the plants.

1. Rutabagas $5
2. Tomatoes $4
3. Cucumbers $4
4. Corn $2
5. Green peas $3
6. Black-eyed peas $5
7. Spinach $5
8. Carrots $3

1. What constraint is Timory concerned with?

2. Which of the plants at the nursery does Timory not need to plant in her mother's new garden?

3. Does Timory have enough money to make the garden she planned on?

   A. Yes

   B. No

Yesterday you learned about the ways that budget can constrain the possible options in a design. Today you will explain what Timory could do in order to make a great garden for her mother despite these constraints.

Directions: Read the text below. Then answer the questions that follow.

1. What is one possible solution to Timory's budget problem? There could be more than one correct answer.

   A. Buy different, cheaper plants not on the original list

   B. Buy more plants at a later date when she has more money

   C. Buy only $18 worth of plants, leaving the spinach off of her list for now

   D. Not plant the garden and forget about it

2. If Timory wants to have this garden planted in the next week, what new constraint would she have?

3. Which plants are the cheapest?

4. If Timory's mother did not care about what plants were in the garden, what 5 plants could Timory buy and still be within her budget?

Yesterday you explained how Timory could find solutions that fit her particular constraints. Today you will take these concepts and apply them to your roller coaster design.

Directions: Read the text below. Then answer the questions that follow.

Today you will spend some time researching possible constraints related to your rollercoaster. Let's imagine a theme park decided to buy your design, but they told you it needed to be built for less than $1,200,000. It might seem like a lot of money, but when you are building something that needs to be both fun and safe, that money can be spent relatively quickly. Read the following questions below and answer them as you research:

1. What is the average cost to build a roller coaster? You can also write a range of costs.

2. Let's pretend the theme park wants your roller coaster to be built out of metal rather than wood. What metals are typically used in roller coasters?

3. What is the cost per foot for this type of metal?

4. Look at your drawings and models of your design. Estimate how many total feet of metal you would need in order to build your design. Include all the support beams, the track, and any other component that would need to be made of metal.

5. Using your answer for question #3, what is the cost of the metal alone if you were to build your roller coaster to scale?

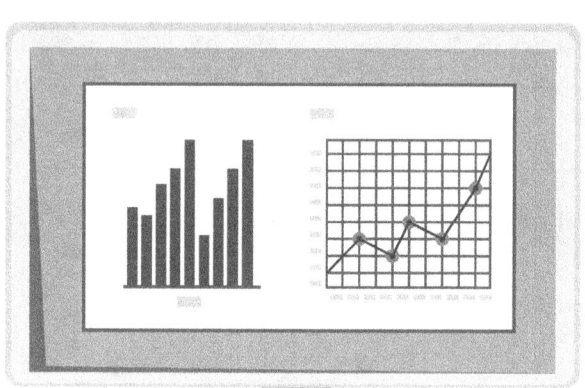

Evaluating, Redesigning, and Modifying

ELABORATING ON THE TOPIC

Yesterday you did some research about budgeting for a rollercoaster. Today you will elaborate on this research and finish out the workbook with a final rollercoaster design!

Directions: Read the text below. Then answer the questions that follow.

1. Based on your research, do you think you could build your roller coaster design within the $1.2 million dollar budget?

2. If you were over budget, what is one thing you could do to alter your design so that it was within budget and also still made of metal like the theme park requested?

3. What is one thing your rollercoaster needs to have in order to make sure it is within the constraints of safety?

4. If your rollercoaster needed to be built in 3 months, would it be possible? Research how long, on average, it takes to build a rollercoaster from start to finish.

5. Did you enjoy designing a roller coaster using the Engineering Design Spiral?

   A. Yes

   B. No

Answer Sheets

To see the answer key to the entire workbook, you can easily download the answer key from our website!

*Due to the high request from parents and teachers, we have removed the answer key from the workbook so you do not need to rip out the answer key while students work on the workbook.

To watch free video explanations go to: **argoprep.com/science6**
OR scan the QR Code:

Place your mouse over the workbook you have, and you will see the "Download Answers" button.

For detailed video instructions on how to access the "Answer Sheets," please scan this QR code.

6th Grade Science: Daily Practice
Workbook | 20 Weeks of Fun

3rd Grade Science: Daily Practice
Workbook | 20 Weeks of Fun...

4th Grade Science: Daily Practice
Workbook | 20 Weeks of Fun...

7th Grade Science: Daily Practice
Workbook | 20 Weeks of Fun...

5th Grade Science: Daily Practice
Workbook | 20 Weeks of Fun...

8th Grade Science: Daily Practice
Workbook | 20 Weeks of Fun...

Kindergarten Science: Daily Practice
Workbook | 20 Weeks of Fun...

1st Grade Science: Daily Practice
Workbook | 20 Weeks of Fun...

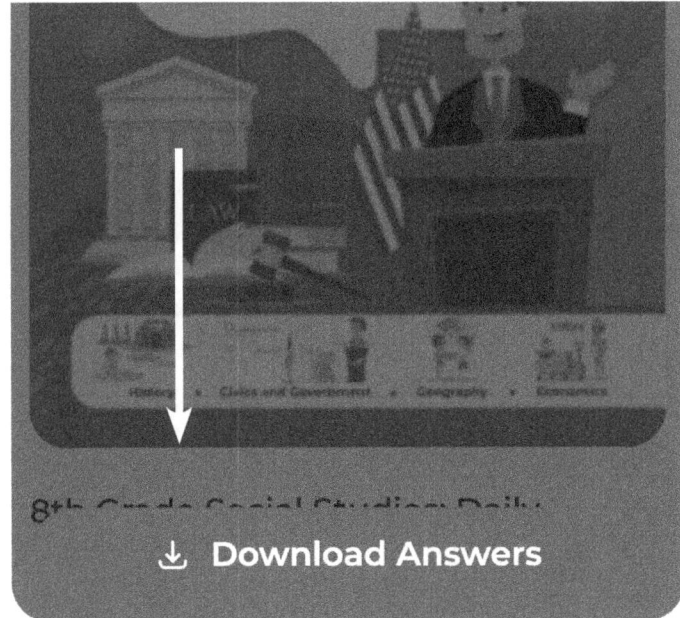

8th Grade Social Studies: Daily

⤓ Download Answers

4th Grade Social Studies:
Practice Workbook